The World's
DUMBEST
CRIMINALS

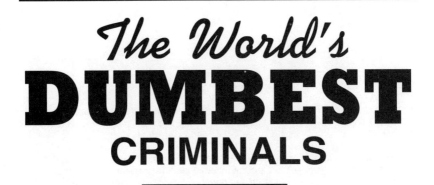

The World's
DUMBEST
CRIMINALS

Based on true stories from law enforcement officials around the world

DANIEL BUTLER AND ALAN RAY

Illustrations by Mike Harris

RUTLEDGE HILL PRESS®

Nashville, Tennessee
A Thomas Nelson Company

The authors have taken great caution to protect the identity of persons depicted in this book. While the crimes depicted are true, the names and gender of the criminals depicted, and some details of the crimes portrayed, may have been changed to safeguard those identities.

Published by Rutledge Hill Press, a Thomas Nelson Company, P.O. Box 141000, Nashville, Tennessee 37214.

Typography by E. T. Lowe

Library of Congress Cataloging-in-Publication Data

Butler, Daniel R., 1951–
    The world's dumbest criminals / Daniel Butler and Alan Ray :
illustrations by Mike Harris.
      p.   cm.
    ISBN 1-55853-541-1
    1. Crime—Case studies. 2. Criminals—Case studies. 3. Crime—
Humor. I. Alan, Ray. II. Title.
    HV6251.B87 1997
    364.1'092'273—dc21
                                                 97-30695
                                                 CIP

Printed in the United States of America

7   8   9 — 05

Table of Contents

To our little ones: Max, Jake, and Baby X (due in February); and John, Sarah, and John Austin (due in January).

And to our wives, Susie and Karen.

We love you.

Acknowledgments

A special thank-you to Robin Howarth, Carl Meisner, the International Police Association, Larry Rose; and to all the officers who have written, e-mailed, faxed, and called.

Introduction

Alan and I have visited motels, cop stations, radio stations, and F.O.P. lodges across America, along the way continually hearing about new and excruciatingly dumb attempts at crime. Now, by Internet, telephone, fax, and mail, we have been around the *world* and back again. Through it all we have learned a lot and laughed even more.

In doing the research for this book, we proved three things:

First: Dumb crime is not just an American phenomenon. It is a universal problem. Dumb criminals are the same the world over, and they make the same mistakes in every culture and kingdom. Their first mistake is always thinking they can get away with it.

Second: Every nation in the world is full of good cops with a great sense of humor. They have to find humor whenever and wherever they can. That's because they have to put up with horrible lies, stupid excuses, and just plain dumb people. Such is the daily lot of cops everywhere. Fortunately, almost all of them have learned to "grin and bear it."

Third: There is no right way to do a wrong thing. Regardless of one's nationality or his home's longitude or latitude, wrong is right is a universal misconception. A Frenchman has no more chance of committing the perfect crime than a Bolivian.

Perhaps American films and television have sold the idea that there is such a thing as the perfect crime. There isn't. This idea of getting something for nothing predates the media and the absurdity of believing in the perfect crime knows no boundaries. That said, keep turning the pages and have some good laughs on the bad guys. Rest assured that readers all over the world will commiserate with you and laugh along right along.

—Daniel Butler

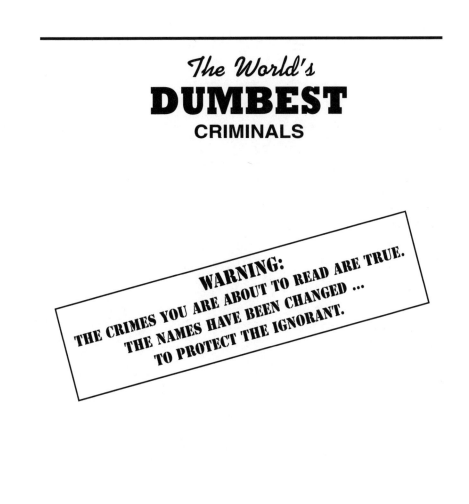

The World's

DUMBEST

CRIMINALS

WARNING:
THE CRIMES YOU ARE ABOUT TO READ ARE TRUE.
THE NAMES HAVE BEEN CHANGED ...
TO PROTECT THE IGNORANT.

Tito's Last Grab

(Spain)

A smash-and-grab artist practices the world's third- or fourth-oldest profession. Ever since merchants began displaying their wares in marketplaces, skilled thieves have executed this lightning-fast form of larceny. With choreographed precision, the smash-and-grab professional will throw a heavy object through a shop's glass window, dodge the flying glass, scoop up all the merchandise he can carry, then sprint for sanctuary—all in less than fifteen seconds.

But times are hard for today's smash-and-grab artists, with Plexiglas and unbreakable windows standing up to their quick assaults and merchants becoming more savvy in what they display and when and where they display it. This selective display strategy made for an interesting robbery in Barcelona, reported to us by retired officer Alfredo Diaz.

We'll call our dumb Spanish criminal Tito the Bandito, or the Barcelona Bungler. Having watched Tito grow up, Officer Diaz couldn't help thinking that our bandito had wasted his great gifts of speed, good hands, and fearlessness. Tito had all the qualities of a great bullfighter, but, instead, he chose a life of easy, ill-gotten gains. Since the age of twelve Tito had been successful at perfecting the smash–and–grab, and he had never been caught. He was something of a legend to the other criminals in the city, but a thorn in Officer Diaz's side.

Tito just could not resist a lovely display of jewels, watches, or silverware; he believed they were all there for his taking. Following each robbery Tito would shower his señoritas with lovely (and, to him, free) gifts. The rest he would sell for cash.

But a señorita will not receive the same gift or even the same type of gift over and over with the same joy and gratitude. This is why Tito stopped at one of the most expensive shoe stores in Barcelona to admire the incredibly expensive designer shoes in the window display. Twisting like a matador, he grabbed a small metal trash bin from the sidewalk, spun it in an tight arc, and released it right into the center of the huge plate-glass window. Tito's hands were so quick that he actually had time to thrust them into his pockets as the glass crashed onto the sidewalk in front of him. Within seconds he had grabbed every shoe in sight and vanished.

Four blocks away, Tito finally slowed down to rest. Ducking behind a restaurant, he sat down to inspect the fine leather and craftsmanship of the shoes.

They were magnificent.

They were supple and soft.

They were colorful and well-made.

They were all for the right foot.

Tito panicked. He kept rifling through his booty, but there was not a left shoe to be found. That's when the policeman tapped him on the shoulder. Tito, the great smash-and-grab artist, had to end his career without ever hearing the other shoe fall.

2 Self-Portrait of a Dumb Criminal

(New Zealand)

Here's the story of an armed robbery that took place at a family-owned food store in western New Zealand. The clerk on duty that night was twenty-two-year-old Danny Wilson. When the police arrived, Wilson told them that a lone gunman had entered the store around 11:30 that evening and had asked to use the rest room.

"I pointed to the door in the back," Wilson said, "and he went in. He stayed in there for about five minutes and when he came out, he was holding a gun. *'Give me all the money now!'* he shouted. Thinkin' I was gonna be shot at any moment, I did as he said."

When Wilson finished telling his story again, one of the officers said to him, "You've told what happened twice now and you've not mentioned a mask or disguise. Did you get a pretty good look at him, then?"

"I guess so."

"So, he wasn't wearing a mask of any sort?"

"No, he wasn't wearing no mask or nothin'."

"Officer Petersen, would you grab a sketch pad and come talk to this young man please?"

The young clerk began to fidget. He looked uneasy.

Officer Petersen took him aside and began asking him questions about the robber.

"I want you to look at some basic face shapes on these cards and tell me which one most fits the robber. Was it round like this one or more narrow?"

"It was thinner, like this one."

"Okay. Now, what can you tell me about the shape of his nose?"

The officer began to sketch as the clerk described in detail the eyes, the type of hair, and the color, even down to the bump on the bridge of his nose. The kid was fascinated as he watched the artist at work. Once in a while he would recall some small detail you wouldn't expect a person with a gun pointed at him to notice.

Twenty minutes later they had a complete composite. Officer Peterson looked at the finished sketch. With a puzzled look, he excused himself and went over to the sergeant in charge. They both looked at the drawing and then mumbled to each other. The clerk began scratching himself. The two officers approached him.

19

"You have an excellent eye for detail, son."

"That was quite a description that you gave to Officer Petersen," added the sergeant.

"Yeah, he's real good."

"Put your hands behind your back. You're under arrest for the robbery of this store."

Unbelievable. The fool was unable to describe any other face, save his own! He confessed that he was the robber. When the arresting officer asked him why, he responded, "I was just being honest!"

The Stooges Go North, Eh?

3

(Canada)

Canadian winters are long and hard, which is why the first warm days of spring find every Canadian fleeing the insanity of cabin fever for the great outdoors.

One such glorious spring day brought a group of five Windsor, Ontario, office workers outside for an ice cream bar during their lunch break. Enjoying the sun, they sat on benches in front of their building, which faced a bank branch office.

Quietly eating their ice cream and listening to the birds chirp, all five coworkers suddenly noticed a dilapidated car pulling up into the bank's driveway. They could clearly see three men in the car. The passenger in the front seat and the gentleman in the back seat quickly pulled ski masks over their heads, hefted handguns, and darted into the bank. The driver shifted the car into reverse and slowly backed up to right in front of the door, where he kept the car running. The five coworkers looked at each other in stunned silence. Before they could move, the two men who had entered the bank came running back out carrying money bags.

One masked man was almost to the car's back door when he stumbled. His hand clenched, his gun fired, and he shot himself in his left foot. The other masked man yelled *"Hit it!"* as he ran behind the car to get to the other back door. The driver obeyed and the car squealed off, *still in reverse,* flattening the second gunman. The driver slammed on the brakes just in time to be cut off by two police cruisers arriving on the scene.

As handcuffs came out and the arrests were made, the five coworkers sat with their mouths agape, staring at the slapstick scene that had taken less than two minutes to play itself out. In less than ten minutes ambulances had taken away the wounded would-be robbers, the police had returned the money to the bank, and break time was over.

Spring Is in the Air

(Hungary)

Look before you leap. Most of us have been familiar with this old adage since childhood. Some of us, as our international nitwit was soon to discover, would do well to heed those words of wisdom.

A robber was being chased through the streets of Budapest by the local constabulary when he ran upstairs to the second story of an abandoned apartment building. With the police only moments behind him, he ran from room to empty room desperately looking for a place to hide.

As he entered another gutted apartment, he closed the door behind him. He could hear the shouts and collective footsteps of the authorities sweeping down the hall and kicking open doors. He was trapped! He ran over to the window and looked down to the street—it was probably twenty-five feet at least, but he had no choice.

He ran back to the door of the apartment just as the police arrived and they began pounding. With his body pressed hard against the door, he tried to hold them back, but the door was giving way. With one long adrenaline-pumped scream, he bolted from the closed door to the open window and, without missing a step, leaped to the street below just as the police entered the room.

Now on any other given day that little leap of faith might have gone unnoticed but not this day. How could he have known that a circus was in town, that their parade had turned the corner and was passing directly beneath him? The good news was he landed on something soft; the bad news, it was a trampoline.

The police entering the upper-floor room saw him disappear from sight as he left the window. Five seconds later they saw him reappear in midair, only this time he was upside down. The second time he appeared, he wasn't quite as high but he was spinning. He didn't appear a third time.

When the police reached the Flying Nut, he was lying in a heap on the sidewalk across the street from the apartment building. He had suffered a dislocated shoulder, along with several contusions and a concussion. He

The good news was he landed on something soft; the bad news, it was a trampoline.

25

was arrested and taken to jail, reminding him that even criminals who soar must eventually return to earth.

His only visitor at the jail we were told, was the owner of the circus who offered him a good paying job if he could repeat the trick twice a night. Perhaps that's an offer he should have jumped at!

For the Freshest Breath Possible

5

(Australia)

An officer in Brisbane brought in a driver for blood-alcohol testing after he apprehended him for erratic driving and smelled alcohol on his breath. Upon failing the field sobriety test, the suspect had become visibly upset. No wonder. He was a professional driver and couldn't afford to lose his license.

In response to the man's request, the officer agreed to let the drunken driver use the station's rest room. No worry there—the bathroom had no windows for purposes of escape. The officer calmly waited for the man outside the door for what seemed like a reasonable time, then decided to investigate.

He found the suspect in front of the sink, foaming at the mouth.

Startled, the officer rushed to the man's assistance, only to discover that the inebriated driver was chewing on a bar of deodorant soap. It took a while to (1) get the soap out of the fool's mouth and (2) to get Mr. Clean to talk. It turns out he only wanted to get any trace of the alcohol smell out of his mouth before taking any more tests.

The blood test showed a blood-alcohol level of .24, well over the legal definition of intoxicated. An Irish Spring level of .36 put him well over the legal definition of "fresh as a daisy."

Breaking and Entering and Floating

6

(Tortola, British Virgin Islands)

On the tropical paradise of Tortola, life is really laid back. Caressed by tropical trade winds, Tortola has the climate and the pace of a sleepy Caribbean island with the predictable combination of super-wealthy tourists and a very poor native population. The stark contrast of a one-room concrete house for a family of six, to the four-million-dollar weekend getaway for a New York couple, is too much of a temptation for some.

One father of four succumbed to the temptation and forced his way into a mansion by the sea. He brought a four-foot burlap sack. In only a few moments he had collected a TV, a VCR, a clock radio, and a video camera. Then he heard someone in the driveway. He dashed out to the deck, from where he noticed a long narrow lap pool overlooking a seventy-foot drop to the rocky beach below.

The thief threw his bag of loot into the bushes and dove into the pool. In a moment, the lights came on as two officers entered the house. They searched room by room and cleared the house, then one officer hit the deck and pool lights.

They both stood and stared. There in the middle of the pool was the intruder totally naked, floating on his back with his eyes closed. His clothes had sunk to the bottom of the pool. The pool was completely lit from below the water. At first, the officers thought they had a homicide or suicide, but as they approached the body they thought they saw him breathing.

"Police officers! Sir, are you okay?"

No response. One officer grabbed a beach ball and lofted it up in the air. It came down perfectly on the floating man's stomach. *Phwaaap!* It scared the thief so badly that he doubled up immediately and began thrashing to stay afloat. He looked down at the pool lights in amazement. With his eyes closed in the water on a moonless night, he thought he was invisible. He's now quite visible, behind bars.

Don't You Hate It When That Happens?

(America)

It was, of course, another beautiful day in Hawaii, and just an ordinary morning at Honolulu's Ala Moana Shopping Center—until a shopper on a mission came hurtling into one of the mall's specialty shops. Grabbing six expensive leather handbags, he was gone almost before the clerk had time to blink. Now, while most sticky-fingered criminals are notoriously fast on their feet, this guy was creating a breeze, although it was his brakes he needed to be concerned about.

The clerk hit the alarm and guards were right behind the handbag snatcher as he bolted through the mall doors and sprinted toward his car in the parking lot. Just as the chase was warming up, however, it screeched to a halt. The guards were mystified when the dumb criminal stopped beside his car and began to weep.

They had to ask, "Why are you crying? Why didn't you try to drive away?"

Pointing inside the car, the thief tearfully explained, "I left my keys in the ignition and locked myself out."

Is That You?

(England)

A pair of teenaged criminals in Liverpool had a good thing going. One would slowly cruise the block in his car while the other broke into a parked car. Their orchestration was such that the driver of the getaway car would ease around a corner just about the time his buddy was ready to hop back in holding a new radio, CD player, or cell phone. Within five minutes they would have the loot fenced for cash and be back on the street, hundreds of pounds richer.

Although aware of the incidents, police were finding this case hard to crack. There were no witnesses, no prints, and no clues, and none of the fences would talk. The only thing left to do was to step up patrols of the area.

One night two undercover officers were cruising a neighborhood at a crawl, checking out a parked car, when the back door of *their* car opened. In hopped a teen with a radio in hand.

"Hit it!" the youth implored. *"Go!"*

The officers looked at each other incredulously, stifled a laugh, and obeyed. They whipped around the block, cuffed their new passenger, and stopped the sedan that was honking its horn loudly. They had caught both perpetrators in the act. But how?

It turns out that the nearsighted point man had forgotten his glasses that night and mistaken the slow-moving officers' car for his accomplice's vehicle.

So the old fish story is true: Sometimes the fish really *do* jump into the boat.

A Washout of a Robbery

9

(Germany)

Even in Germany the old saying, "People don't plan to fail; they fail to plan," holds true. But our research shows us that even the best-laid criminal plan still has a good chance of failing miserably. Take for example the Terrible Tunnelers of Hamburg. This dastardly duo plotted and planned their crime for months. They were going to execute the perfect bank robbery. No detail would be overlooked.

With intense study and crafty use of aliases and fake documents, the two had amassed a mountain of information for their heist, including the blueprints of the bank building and the surrounding buildings, a schematic of the alarm system, delivery and pick-up information from the armored car company, deposit and transfer schedules, and even some of the security codes from the bank itself.

These guys had done their homework, and the plan was flawless. They would dig into the basement of the bank from an adjoining building so as to avoid the alarm system. Then they would disable the security system from the inside and shuttle all the cash and the valuables from the safe deposit boxes through the tunnel to two getaway vehicles that would then head out in two different directions. It would be morning before the theft was discovered: By then they would be a full continent away.

Timing was everything, and the robbers' timing was perfect. The deposits were at their maximum. The vault was full. With the precision of a drill team, they began the theft that they had rehearsed countless times. Undetected, they slipped into the basement of the insurance company office next door to the bank and silently laid out their tools. Using high-powered drills wrapped in towels (to silence them), the sub-dynamic duo drilled holes in the basement wall at key spots, determined mathematically. Then the mastermind of the operation hefted a twenty-pound sledgehammer for the single well-placed blow that would crumble the wall and put them inside the bank.

The two genius robbers exchanged a smile, and then he swung. *Wham!* The wall cracked perfectly. Sections of

The moral of this story: Always call before you dig.

plaster and wood gave way. Their chain reaction had begun. So far, so good.

So long.

Suddenly and shockingly, they were engulfed in a huge wall of water gushing from the gaping hole they had just put in the largest artery of the city's water main. In their detailed planning, the Terrible Tunnelers had neglected to check out the water company.

The moral of this story: Always call before you dig. The Terrible Tunnelers almost drowned in the deluge they had created, but the police arrived just in time to rescue them.

The Dumbest Slow-Motion Crash in Canadian History

10

(Canada)

It happened in Hamilton, Ontario. Officer Rob Tate and four other officers, called to the scene of a street shooting, had immediately secured it to keep onlookers back. A yellow "Police Line: Do Not Cross" tape stretched across the street. Two marked patrol cars sat diagonally at the curb with their lights flashing, and an unmarked detective car was parked broadside in the street. A crowd of forty to fifty people had gathered to see what was going on.

All in all, it was quite a conspicuous scene. But not conspicuous enough for the geezer who came careening around the corner just then in his '88 Buick. He was cruising at, oh, five miles per hour. Everyone turned and noticed the solid old car as it picked up speed (to maybe nine miles per hour), but no one was really worried. Surely he saw the crime scene. How could he miss the crowd, the cars, and the bright flashing lights?

Sure enough, he slowed down. He was only driving about six miles per hour when he drove into the yellow tape, which slowly pulled tight and snapped just as the Buick's nose crunched into the side of the detective's car. Like a turtle with a mission, that car just kept inching forward as the old gentleman squinted to see what was slowing him down. Tate, the other officers, and the crowd just had to laugh. It was one of those weird moments when everyone knows something dumb is about to happen—and it does.

Afterward, the elderly driver protested that officers had hung the tape at the wrong height. And maybe they had. After all, it was just high enough to stretch out across his windshield and break right in front of his face.

A Flare for Smuggling

(Puerto Rico)

It takes a pirate's heart and steady nerves to be a drug smuggler. Pepe Orlando had neither.

On his first job he had loaded a small airplane with so much pot that he flew only ten feet off the ground before crashing into the trees at the end of the homemade runway. All Orlando had to do this time, for his second job, was sit out in international waters and wait for the pickup boat to arrive.

Eight hours passed and there was no sign of them. He glanced at his watch—2:00 A.M. Where were they? In another four hours it would be daylight. Orlando didn't want to be sitting on the open ocean in a small boat with eight hundred pounds of marijuana on board. And it was getting foggy.

Around 4:30 A.M. visibility was still poor. On the edge of panic, he could make out the silhouette of a boat. It was passing back and forth, probably looking for him. He ran out onto deck.

"Hey! Hey, come back! Over here!" he yelled, jumping up and down and flapping his arms. Then he remembered—the flare gun! He ran to his tackle box, opened the lid, lifted out the tray, and grabbed the gun, which had been tangled up in a bunch of loose fishing gear.

As he ran toward the bow of the boat with gun in hand, Orlando stepped on a wad of fish line hanging from the gun. In that moment his arm was yanked down and, with his finger on the trigger, he fired a flare—right into the cabin. Soon, flames were racing from the cabin onto the deck and leaping ten feet high.

Well, the "pickup boat" by now had turned around and was racing back toward him with sirens blaring. What he had mistaken for his contact ship in the fog was actually the Coast Guard, patrolling international waters for smugglers like Orlando.

DUMB CRIMINAL QUIZ NO. 630

How well do you know the dumb criminal mind?

Complete this sentence: When we were taping an episode of *America's Dumbest Criminals* one day, a man we had hired to play a dumb criminal drove up to the set . . .

A. . . . with his new Hollywood agent.

B. . . . in a spanking new stretch limo.

C. . . . in a stolen car.

D. . . . drunker than a skunk.

The correct answer, believe it or not, is C. Security police on hand noticed the smashed wing vent and ran the tag number. Stolen! The cops, however, sensitive to our tight production schedule, held off arresting the guy until after his scene was shot.

12 Who You Gonna Call?

(America)

An officer in Washington, D.C., answered the call about a car break-in along one of the main streets. He arrived at the scene to find the automobile in question, its trunk obviously jimmied, but no owner. Since the car was parked outside a bar, the officer stepped in to see if the car's owner was inside. He had to talk to several patrons before he finally found his man—who proved to be highly indignant.

"Well, it's about time. I called half an hour ago."

The officer pointed out that it had only been twelve minutes since his call and that he had been looking for the car owner for about five minutes. Then he asked the gentleman what exactly had been taken from his car.

"Ten thousand dollars in cash."

"Could you repeat that, sir?"

"Ten thousand dollars in cash, from my trunk."

The officer noted the amount and asked the man to show him the car. The owner stepped outside with the officer and directed him to the back of his car. The trunk's bent metal lid and twisted lock were telltale signs that a crowbar had been used to pry the trunk open.

"Would you open the trunk, sir?"

The owner didn't answer.

"Sir, would you open the trunk?"

"Why?" The owner looked seriously concerned about something.

"Well, sir, to file a report, I need to establish all the facts—such as the fact that the money isn't in the trunk now."

The car's owner thought for a moment, paced a bit, then asked the officer, "So if I open the trunk, you're just going to look for the money?"

"I need to establish that the money isn't in there. Yes, sir."

The car's owner thought a bit more and finally relented. He unlocked the trunk and stepped back. The officer's eyes landed immediately on a clear plastic bag containing approximately ten pounds of marijuana.

"Sir, you're under arrest for possession of a controlled substance."

"You can't do that! You said you were only looking for the money, and the money isn't there."

"Well, sir, the marijuana is in plain sight and, as an officer of the law, I cannot ignore evidence of a crime."

The man was furious. "Well, I suppose you're going to bust me for the cocaine under the front floor mat, too."

The officer couldn't believe his ears. "No, sir. I'll call a judge for a search warrant and then, if I find cocaine under the front floor mat, I'll bust you for that, too."

He did. The final count was ten pounds of marijuana, five grams of cocaine, one gallon of moonshine . . . and one very indignant dumb criminal, in custody.

Have a dumb day!

Double Steal

(Colombia)

When retired Army MP Richard Berry went to Bogotá to visit an old army buddy, he was told this story of a car thief who had a twisted sense of right and wrong.

While cruising on routine patrol one Saturday night, an officer was flagged down in the middle of the street by a woman screaming at the top of her lungs and frantically waving both arms.

"What's the trouble?" the concerned officer asked.

"They stole my car! That's them in the green car!"

The officer spotted the car only a block away.

"Is that the car right there?" he said, asking for confirmation.

"Yes, yes. I ran into my friend's house for two minutes and when I came out they were driving away!"

"Get in!" said the officer.

With the little green car still in view, the officer, with the victim seated next to him, began his pursuit. After several high-speed moments, the stolen automobile was finally stopped with the assistance of several other police units. The three men inside were arrested and charged with multiple violations.

Now, you would think that this would be the end of the story, but *nooooo.* During the pursuit, the officer gave the dispatcher a complete description of the car, including the license plate number. When the dispatcher ran the tag number, it came back as a stolen vehicle.

Now that's odd, thought the cop. He turned to the lady. "Did you report this car stolen before you flagged me down?"

"No, how could I? It happened just as you pulled up."

"That's what I was thinking," the officer told her. "Let me ask you this. Is that your car?"

"No," she replied matter-of-factly. "I stole it."

Stunned, the policeman shook his head. "You stole it? When?"

"An hour ago. I was going to return it. I just needed a ride to go see my friend."

The officer could see the big picture starting to come into focus. "Did you steal this car to go buy dope?" he asked.

"Yes, I did. So what?"

"So what? So you're under arrest for stealing a car. And you've probably got some dope on you right now."

Amazingly, the thief-victim seemed unconcerned about the dope and returned to the subject of the car.

"You can't arrest me for stealing that car!" she shouted. "They took it last. *They're* the ones with a stolen car, not me."

"Wait a minute. You believe because they stole it from you, it cancels out the fact that you stole it to begin with?"

"Right!"

"Wrong!"

The woman was arrested and charged with car theft. When she was searched at the jail, cocaine was found on her person and additional charges were filed.

Honesty Is the Best Policy

(Belgium)

A man suspected of robbing a jewelry store in Liège was arrested, booked, and arraigned for trial, all the while protesting that he was innocent.

Finally, his day in court arrived, and the man had a chance to prove his claim. To everyone's astonishment, he produced an ironclad alibi, which the police later confirmed:

"Your honor, I could not have robbed that jewelry store because at *that* time on *that* day, I was breaking into a school across town."

You know what happened next. Police arrested him for breaking into the school.

Hot Dip Pursuit

(Australia)

An officer making his rounds behind the wheel in Sydney fell in behind a suspicious-looking car. The officer's interest had been aroused by the license plate that had been shoved haphazardly into the car's back window. A quick radio call revealed that the plate belonged to a different make and model of vehicle.

Just as the officer was flicking on his lights and siren, he realized he had been made. The door to the car flew open, and the driver took off on foot into a nearby neighborhood. By the time the officer had radioed his position and jumped out of his car to give chase, the suspect had a good fifty-foot head start.

It was the proliferation of backyard fences that enabled the officer to close the gap. With every yard, the suspect lost more of his lead. The suspect would scale one fence,

But there was one problem: Our dumb criminal couldn't swim.

tumble over to the other side, pull himself to his feet, and keep on truckin'. This went on for five backyard fences, with the officer gaining ground each time. He was almost within an arm's length when the suspect launched himself over a six-foot privacy fence. Then came the splash—and the screams.

Peering over the top of the fence, the officer started laughing as he watched his prey flailing helplessly in the beautifully landscaped swimming pool.

Now, a nice, cool dip might sound refreshing after a bit of hot pursuit, but there was one problem: Our dumb criminal couldn't swim. Instead of enjoying his dunking, he was gurgling, "Save me, please. Officer, help!"

Who says there's never a cop around when you need one?

16 The Safety-First Elf

(Canada)

Office parties in the weeks leading up to Christmas are known for producing many drivers who have imbibed an excess of Yuletide cheer. Constable Peter Smidt of the Royal Canadian Mounted Police Highway Patrol in Vancouver, British Columbia, encountered just such an inebriated Christmas elf late one December night.

When he received a radio call about a Wrong Way Charlie traveling east in the westbound lane of the interstate, Smidt kicked on his lights and sirens and hurried toward the scene, hoping to head off the misdirected driver before he reached a nearby tunnel. Too late. Miraculously, though, the misdirected driver had made it through unscathed.

Constable Smidt pulled the man over and asked him what he thought that two-lane road "just over there" was.

The obviously inebriated man sagely answered, "Why, that is a road going in the same direction I am." Then he began to fumble through his wallet and glove compartment for his driver's license and vehicle registration—while carrying on a continuous conversation with someone in the seat next to him.

Constable Smidt was surprised; he had seen only one person in the car when he stopped it. Now he bent over and scanned the interior of the vehicle. No one was there except the fragrant driver.

"Who are you talking to, sir?" Smidt politely asked.

"My wife, of course," the man responded, confusion washing over his face only when Smidt pointed to the empty passenger seat.

It turned out that Wrong Way had indeed been to an office party and had departed with his wife. Then he had dropped her off at home and driven away, apparently forgetting not only where he was going but also the fact that she was no longer with him.

He was not too drunk, however, to remember his profession. When asked to state his occupation for the arrest report, he proudly reported that he worked for the government—as a safety engineer.

Tinted and Towed

(Ireland)

Have you ever heard the wail of a home security-system alarm? They are loud and obnoxious, but the unfortunate truth is that they rarely prevent a break-in.

Such was the case in a wealthy suburb of Dublin a few years ago, where a woman heard that shriek of an alarm emanating from her neighbor's house. She ran to her front window and saw a German-made car with tinted windows speeding away. She immediately called the *gardai* (Celtic for *policeman*), and an officer took down a description of the car. Within moments, the vehicle was the object of a manhunt that seemed to include almost every cop in Ireland.

About a half-hour later, a detective returning from taking the homeowner's statement tried to pull into the police station parking lot, but a certain German-made car with tinted windows was blocking the driveway. *This was too easy,* he thought. Surely the burglar wouldn't just turn himself in. He was right.

Moments later, the bad guy came strolling out of the pawnshop across the street, whistling a happy tune and counting his money. He hopped into his car and turned the key. That's when the police closed in and apprehended him. Then they took him, oh, a good ten feet into the station for booking.

It turned out that the tinted windows were *so* dark that this particular dumb criminal couldn't see the police station sign glowing in the night, right above his parked car.

18 My Karma Ran over My Dogma

(Syria)

The mindless mugger-to-be was Habib Rasham, who stood quietly in the darkened alley as he watched his approaching prey. Watching and waiting was nothing new to our foreign felon. With a large stick in hand, he would hide until his unsuspecting victim walked past, then step up quietly behind him, strike him over the head, and steal the victim's money.

Tonight was no exception. As Rasham stood in the darkness against the wall, a man passed within five feet of him. Out of the darkness he crept up behind the man and dealt him a sharp rap on the back of his head. The victim dropped facedown into the alley way.

Quickly, Rasham rifled through the man's pockets. In the back pocket he found a wallet. Just as the victim began to stir back to consciousness, two men entered the alley and shouted at Rasham, who took off running. In a flash he was down the alley, onto the street, and ambling along, trying to blend in with other pedestrians.

As Rasham walked along, he pulled out the stolen wallet and began removing the contents. First the money, then the identification. Suddenly, he stopped. *It couldn't be.* The color drained from his face. Not only did he know his victim, he *lived* with him. Rasham's karma had finally caught up with him. *He had just mugged his own father!* He sprinted back to the alley. No one was there. He looked down the street. Aha, there he was! As Rasham approached his father, the two men who had seen him shouted, *"That's him!"* Still holding his father's wallet, Rasham was immediately set upon by an angry crowd.

This Rasham family minireunion was not a pretty sight. Rasham was thoroughly trounced, probably disowned, and definitely arrested!

19 The World's Fastest Cop

(America)

It was a typical cold night outside Fairbanks, Alaska, when Officer Mike Smith noticed a car's headlights peering out from a roadside snowbank—a fairly routine sight in Alaska in the winter. Smith lit a flare and started down to give assistance. Then he realized that the inebriated driver had no idea he was wedged into an embankment. He must have thought he was in a heck of a blizzard because he was staring intently at the snow ahead, driving for all he was worth. His foot was on the gas, and the rear tires were spinning as the car slid slightly from side to side.

Smith couldn't resist: He positioned himself just behind the driver's side window and began to run in place. He rapped on the glass with his flashlight.

The driver did a perfect double take and sped up; so

did Smith. Sprinting in place, Smith again tapped the window. This time the driver relented and "stopped" his car.

When the driver's case came before the magistrate, the judge asked, "Are you guilty as charged?"

The man looked forlornly at the judge and said, "I must be, your honor. The officer chased me down on foot!"

20 The "Mail the Mail" Man

(Canada)

Some criminals are so dumb they outsmart themselves. Case in point: Rene DeLeon, a Canadian postal worker, who discovered that being a mail carrier wasn't all it was cracked up to be with all those days of heavy snow, strong wind, and bitterly cold temperatures.

DeLeon hadn't been working twenty minutes one such day when he decided a change was needed. Outside, he could smoke a joint and no one would be the wiser. He cut through the park and stood behind a large maple tree to block the wind. A friend who had just returned from a Jamaican vacation had given some pot to him with assurances that, after smoking it, DeLeon's vision would be enhanced. He was so right. After just three puffs DeLeon began to see the world around him in a different light.

By the time he'd smoked the rest of the bomber he had

reached Nirvana—a state of pure bliss. Then it struck him—like lightning: He would never have to work again. He could still collect a paycheck. *Mail the mail!* That was it. It was so simple, so pure. Why hadn't he thought of this before?

DeLeon ran to the nearest public mail box and, with no one looking, stood in front of it and began to deposit his route. This done, he went home to enjoy the rest of the day in his nice warm bed.

Late afternoon, the phone startled Rene DeLeon awake. It was his immediate supervisor and *his* supervisor on the phone. He was wanted at the post office, *pronto!*

DeLeon was still groggy as he entered the bosses' office. The meeting was very brief. Facing possible federal prosecution, DeLeon offered no resistance.

"Any chance of a career with the post office," they assured him, "has just gone up in smoke!"

21 The Great Train Robbery

(Switzerland)

Only one train makes its way up the steep Alpine slopes to the little storybook village of Wengen, and it's a tiny one, with just enough room in the passenger cars for one seat on either side of the aisle. The Wengen station is also tiny, just a single track and a miniscule platform.

But none of this mattered to the pair of thieves who took the last train up from the valley one evening near sunset. All they cared about was that the train would leave Wengen for the two villages above it on the mountain and then come right back down the mountain, stopping in Wengen just one hour later. That hour would give them just enough time.

Once off the train in Wengen, the dual dummkopfs headed directly for the village toy store. They waited patiently outside until the owner locked up and walked away, then they hurried to break in through a back window. Within ten minutes they were walking back toward the train station with two armloads of expensive model railroad sets.

They boarded the train and smiled broadly at the conductor, who congratulated them on their fine purchases. They laughed as he continued down the aisle into the next car; they had actually pulled it off! Their faces fell, however, when the train reached Interlochen in the valley below and they saw two police officers waiting for them. Their theft shouldn't have been discovered until morning. What had gone wrong?

The detail they had overlooked was a significant date in the toy-store owner's life—his wedding anniversary. He and his wife had boarded another car on the same train for an anniversary dinner in Interlochen. And when his friend, the conductor, offered congratulations on his big sale, he insisted he had sold no trains that day. That's when the conductor, who had watched the men get off empty-handed and reboard with armloads of trains, put two and two together and wired ahead for the police.

The next day's headlines gave appropriate if misleading credit: "Great Train Robbery Foiled by Quick-Thinking Conductor."

Stickin' to the Job

(America)

Here's the story of the man with the plan to get high and who stuck to his plan. In Baton Rouge, Loggins Taylor had just finished inhaling his last tube of glue. The tube was empty and so were his pockets (and, presumably, his head), but he was still flying with no desire to land. It was the middle of the night and he was desperate.

Idea! Less than three blocks away was the mother ship— a glue factory. Fifteen minutes later Taylor was climbing through a broken warehouse window.

Once inside, he was awestruck. There was more glue here than he'd ever imagined. There was white glue, brown glue, wood glue, metal glue, and airplane glue. His heart pounded. He ran over to a fifty-five-gallon drum of airplane glue and quickly pried the lid off. The fumes

"Do you know you pulled a barrel of glue over on yourself?"

67

rushed out. With both hands on the rim of the barrel he lowered his face and inhaled deeply several times.

He got high.

He got sick.

As his knees buckled, he gripped the barrel tighter to keep from falling. Then he blacked out.

After countless hours, Taylor started coming to. He could hear voices. He opened his left eye. He could see feet, lots of feet. Why wouldn't his right eye open? Where was he and why couldn't he move?

"Just take it easy, pal. We're gonna get you out," came a voice from above.

A policeman, his face turned sideways, lowered himself into Glue Man's view.

"You're stuck to a warehouse floor!" the officer told him, trying hard not to laugh. "Do you know you pulled a barrel of glue over on yourself? You don't look so good."

Taylor couldn't raise his head. The right side of his face was glued tight to the floor, as were his body and both arms. Taylor's legs were crossed and glued to each other. He could hear scraping and picking sounds. And laughter.

It took more than three hours to peel Taylor from the floor. He was arrested, led away in handcuffs, and is now *stuck* in jail.

Not My Brother-in-Law-to-Be's Keeper

(Canada)

If and when you plan to pull off a burglary, be sure to keep track of where your relatives are. There's nothing more embarrassing than running into members of your own family while you're committing a crime—unless it's running into your future in-laws while you're in the act of stealing their neighbor's stuff.

George McMillan was sitting in his Toronto apartment, watching TV and minding his own business, when a familiar face walked by his back door. George thought idly that the passerby looked a lot like his sister's boyfriend. Then the guy strolled back by, pulling a ten-speed bicycle, and George was sure: It was his brother-in-law-to-be, all right.

George assumed he was simply borrowing a bike from a friend—until the neighbor started yelling. Then George realized he had just witnessed a crime, and he knew exactly who the criminal was!

"I'll get your bike back," George told the frantic neighbor. He knew exactly where to go. Sure enough, the dummy-in-law-to-be was at home readjusting the seat of his newly acquired bicycle. With loot and culprit in tow, George returned to his apartment, where his neighbor and the Mounties met him. The thief went from possible in-law to outlaw.

Teacher's Pet

(Japan)

Women are assuming new roles in modern Japan. Men and women alike compete for the same jobs for the first time in the history of this great country. Some Japanese men, however, are not that excited about the gals' new presence in the work force.

"Not too excited" is too mild to describe the feelings of one man, Ito Tanaka, a teller in a downtown Tokyo bank. His supervisor had hired a very attractive, very young, very inexperienced trainee to work with him at his window. He was to mentor this new teller and acquaint her with the job. The teller resented her.

As he handled transactions, the veteran male teller totally ignored the trainee. The trainee occasionally asked questions, only to receive a short and sharp response. At lunch time, the teller was telling the young woman where she could eat and when she should be back to punch in, when he was interrupted by his supervisor.

"I'd like Ms. Li to keep the window open by herself and take a late lunch. You may run along." The teller was appalled. This was *his* window. That was *his* cash drawer. *His* customers came to *his* window.

Ms. Li managed fine with simple deposits and withdrawals during the first twenty minutes. She had paid close attention and, with little or no mentoring, she was doing quite well. At least until she was robbed.

The next man in line was wearing a ski mask and appeared to have a gun in his pocket. He demanded the money in a hushed, angry whisper.

"Open the drawer and look normal," he said. "I want all of the paper bills, including the ten-thousand-yen notes." The woman fumbled with the money, spilling yen all over the floor.

"Pick it up! The larger bills are on the left!"

She did her best to follow his instructions.

"Where are the ten-thousand-yen notes? Can't you remember anything, Ms. Li? I told you those are kept under the cash drawer."

Oops!

The bank officer and several tellers restrained the teller-robber, Mr. Tanaka, until police arrived.

Don't Leave the Crime Scene without It

25

(Germany)

A particular photography shop in Frankfurt was known for offering the finest and most expensive cameras, lenses, and photographic accessories in the city—a gold mine of an inventory. Accordingly, the proprietor had taken great pains in setting up store security. So even when a customer swept up an armful of cameras and ran, the owner wasn't too concerned.

Sure, the guy had just scooped up more than two thousand deutsche marks' worth of merchandise. But the owner had an ace up his sleeve: he had just taken the dummy's passport photos and written down the name and address so he could send the photos when they were ready.

Now he just called police and had *them* deliver the photos to his dumb criminal customer. He even let them keep the photos to use as mug shots.

STRANGE BUT TRUE:

Actual Canadian Laws

(Canada)

Roland Haley retired as a senior constable with the Ontario Provincial Police and found himself with a bit of time on his hands. So Roland set out to make a list of all the laws on the books that he thought were silly. Here's the beginning of Roland's list:

- In Calgary it is against the law to throw snowballs without the authorization of the mayor or the city council.

- In Edmonton all bicycle riders must signal with their arm before making a turn. But a bicycle rider must keep both hands on the handlebars at all times.

- In Ottawa it is illegal for children to eat ice cream cones on the streets on the Sabbath.

- In Saskatoon it is illegal to catch fish with your hands.

- In Toronto it is against the law to saw wood or wash your car on a city street.

- In Victoria you are not allowed to wear a bathing suit while "loitering, playing, or indulging in a sunbath" in any park or on the beach.

- In Windsor you are not allowed to play a musical instrument in a public park.

- In Winnipeg a bylaw forbids anyone from striking the sidewalk with a metal object.

- In Burnaby all dogs must be under control by 10:00 P.M. or the owners will be punished.

- In British Columbia anyone interrupting a meeting of the British Columbia Grasshopper Control Committee can be arrested.

- In Alberta it is against the law for a man to drink with a woman in a beer parlor.

And Roland's just getting warmed up.

26 Calling All Car

(Peru)

In the village of San Luis in the mountainous region of Peru, there was a police force of one. A lone man had been the only law-enforcement officer there for twenty years. While governments changed, Roberto Suarez remained.

After two decades of service, Suarez finally got what he wanted—a police car with a radio. But a two-way radio is useless in San Luis. It wouldn't even reach the next province. So Suarez would pretend to use the radio. This he did for three days—until the radio was stolen.

Now Suarez had a very good reason to get another radio—so he could call the guy who had stolen his first radio. That's one criminal Suarez hoped would be dumb enough to keep in touch.

Grind This, Pal

27

(Italy)

Organ grinders with trained monkeys are a fixture of literature, art, and opera. There never were a large number of people practicing the profession—today there are almost none. But in Brindisi, a young man recently took up the craft, much to the delight of the children and tourists. He added great local color to the town square.

At night, however, the organ grinder and his monkey had another life. The organ grinder would force his hairy companion to dive into mailboxes and bring out handfuls of envelopes. The trick also worked with bank night depositories and bags of money.

Local police were stumped. In each case, there was no forced entry, no sign of entry at all. No fingerprints and no clues. The organ grinder was getting rich, but the monkey was getting ticked.

The monkey had had enough.

The monkey had had enough. When the organ grinder sent the monkey through a vent in a restaurant to raid the cash register, the monkey saw his chance. The organ grinder waited below the vent for what seemed like forever. Still no monkey. Finally, the little monkey appeared in the vent to a torrent of epithets from his master. One little hand held out a wad of cash, then the other little hand produced a hand gun he had found behind the cash drawer. *Blam!* The little monkey nailed his master in the arm and skittered away.

The organ grinder tried to convince the police that he had stopped the robber and struggled with him to get the money and a nasty flesh wound. That's when the monkey returned with the gun. The organ grinder screamed and tried to run, sure that the monkey would finish him off. But the police disarmed the little fella. The organ grinder is still doing time grinding rocks instead of tunes, and the monkey works in school outreach as the police force's mascot.

28 Present Company Excluded

(America)

Okay, so this one isn't really about a dumb criminal, but it does involve a crime, and it sure made at least one person feel pretty dumb.

Two officers in Burlington, Vermont, were taking a report from a victim of domestic violence, who explained that her abusive boyfriend had fled the scene in his "stupid ol' truck." The officers asked her to be more specific in describing the vehicle.

"It's one of those big, stupid trucks that looks like a toy, a big silly toy," she sputtered.

One officer swallowed a chuckle because he knew the officer standing right next to him had exactly such a truck. In fact, it was his pride and joy. He spent every spare minute and every spare dollar on it. He even had a name for it.

"They even give the stupid trucks names," she spat. "He spent all this money on that dumb truck, and then he'd go and drive it in the mud. Stupid. Men that have trucks like that are insecure, I tell you. They're just little short men trying to be big."

The officer let her go on while he watched his slightly built partner squirm, still not saying a word.

"They're just immature, stupid, little men," she went on. "You oughta put 'em all in jail before they do something worse than spend all their money buying a big, stupid truck."

"I couldn't agree . . . with you more, ma'am." The officer choked back laughter as his partner finally turned and silently stalked back to the patrol car.

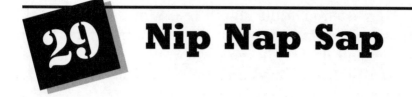

Nip Nap Sap

(Australia)

A deputy in Melbourne answered a call from a man who could only whisper his address into the phone. Responding immediately, the deputy was surprised to find the householders outside, hiding in the bushes. "The bad guy is in our den, asleep," the husband explained. "We hid out here in case he woke up before you arrived."

The deputy called for backup, and two officers soon arrived on the scene to initiate the search. Sure enough, there was the cat burglar curled up in the den—purring in alcoholic slumber next to the wet bar.

The suspect confirmed the officers' suspicions the next day after he had slept off a wicked drunk and was moaning from an equally wicked hangover. He had only begun ransacking the house when he discovered that the owners' bar was stocked with exotic liquors and beers

The owners' bar was stocked with exotic liquors and beers from around the world.

from around the world. Well, this was too good to pass up, so our dumb criminal decided to have just one little taste of the light, fruity, and yet incredibly potent English elderberry wine. While enjoying his first taste of elderberry he noticed some Greek ouzo, another drink he had never tasted. The ouzo left him feeling warm and adventurous, so why not try the unique flavor of dandelion liqueur . . . and then some ice cold chili pepper-flavored beer from Texas . . . and well, you get the picture. He was head down at the bar by the time the householders arrived home.

Maybe we have a new crime deterrent here. Because many studies have found that a vast majority of crimes are committed under the influence of alcohol, why not apply that knowledge and create the dumb-criminal equivalent of a roach motel? The dumb criminal is attracted to the wet bar like a moth to a flame. He sits down and has a nip. Then he simply naps until the police come around to collect him—all nice and cozy, ready for his stretch in jail.

The Thinking Fellow Calls a Yellow

(Canada)

Constable P. Milne of the New Westminster police in British Columbia had a run-in with an unusual bandit near Burnaby one night.

It seems this young fellow had broken into a house and stolen several items, but he didn't have a getaway car. Undaunted, he called a cab. Now, you may think that *this* was the fatal flaw in his criminal plan. As it turned out, however, this Einstein of crime was just getting warmed up.

After the criminal had loaded all his loot into the cab, he climbed in and gave the driver the address of a convenience store. When they arrived, the easy-riding thief asked his cabbie to wait, then proceeded to go inside, pull a pellet gun on the clerk, and demand all the money in the register. The cool clerk simply called the police and then let Sticky Fingers do his thing. He took the money, grabbed a few packs of cigarettes, and headed back to his waiting taxi—where he gave the now-nervous cabbie the address of *another* store.

They headed off again. What the rider didn't notice, however, was the patrol car creeping along behind them. The cabbie noticed it, though. After going a few blocks, he suddenly slammed his taxi into park, ducked down, and rolled out of the front seat just as the law officers surrounded the cab. The cabbie was grateful to be alive, even if he did get stiffed on both fare and tip.

A Fistful of Yen

(China)

An elderly Chinese paymaster was doling out a week's pay to a long line of very disgruntled workers. One by one, they would slouch up to the paymaster's table, then slink off with their small bags of coins. No one ever said thank-you. Many spit and cursed. And the grinning, insolent young man near the end of the line had even worse intentions. When his turn came, he simply grabbed the paymaster's large bag of coins and disappeared into the forest. No one else would get paid that day.

The paymaster was deeply distressed, for it was not the first time he had been robbed, and he could think of no way to prevent such thefts—until an idea occurred to him. Kneeling at his drawing table, he sketched a wooden box just large enough for a man to sit at a table inside it. The box had one door, at the rear, and a kind of latticework in front to allow the person inside to see out. Below the lattice, at about tabletop height, was a narrow slot.

The following Friday, the paymaster was sitting cheerfully in a booth made to this design. For each worker, he would smooth the coins out flat in the bag and slide them out the slot. Inevitably, of course, a worker became bold and thrust his hand through the narrow slot, grabbing several bags of money. But then he was stuck, because his hand wouldn't fit through the slot while he held the bags. A soldier beside the box lifted his ax. The larcenous worker had to drop the money, flatten his hand, and yank it quickly out to avoid losing it altogether.

The lesson was not lost on the crowd. The paymaster had no more trouble with payroll theft. And the idea eventually caught on around the world. Tonight, in fact, when you pay through the slot at the all-night convenience store with the bulletproof glass, remember the Chinese paymaster who designed it.

Oh, yes, remember to move your hand quickly.

The Magic Answer Sheet

32

(America)

A man whom Officer Will O'Diear had stopped for driving under the influence in a southeastern city seemed quite anxious about what would happen to him next. During the course of his arrest, transportation to jail, and booking, he kept asking the same four questions: 1) "Why was I arrested?" 2) "What happened to my car?" 3) "How long will I be in jail?" and 4) "How much is this going to cost me?"

Each time he asked these questions, Officer O'Diear would answer them. Five minutes later, the drunk would forget and ask them all over again. All this was becoming very tiresome until O'Diear had an inspiration.

First, he wrote down the answers to the four questions on a piece of paper. Then he explained to the whining drunk that he was a magician. "I would be willing to share a special piece of magic with you if you'll promise to follow my instructions to the letter."

The drunk looked at the officer intently and nodded his head rapidly up and down. Then the officer held up his paper.

"This is a magic piece of paper. It has all the answers to life's most important questions on it. All you have to do is concentrate hard on your question, then open the paper, and the answer will be there. But you've got to have faith and not ask me or anyone else until you've asked the magic answer sheet." The drunk nodded solemnly and took the paper from the officer.

A few minutes later, O'Diear again heard those familiar words, "Hey, Officer, why . . . ?"

O'Diear just looked at the man. "Did you check with the magic answer sheet?"

The prisoner's eyes got very big, and he slipped the paper out of his sock. He carefully unfolded it as he closed his eyes tight, concentrating on his question. Then he slowly opened his eyes, peered at the sheet, and whooped with pleasure: "It works!"

Chauffeur Driven, with Locked-in Freshness

33

(Germany)

An armored car driver in Hamburg was making his usual round of pick-ups at the end of the day. Pleased that they were ahead of schedule, he whistled as he waited for his assistant to come back with the money bags from the last bank.

Suddenly, a lone gunman appeared. "Step aside, if you know what's good for you."

The driver complied. The gunman stepped into the vault of the armored car, his gun still trained on the driver. When he turned to face the stacks of cash, however, the driver slammed the heavy-gauge steel door shut. *Clank!*

When the assistant returned, the driver casually told him to ride up front, explaining, "I just need to drop something off." Within minutes they were at the police station, where the cops happily took custody of the uninvited cargo.

I Light Up My Life

34

(Australia)

When Harry Eggers of Perth ran out of gas, he didn't worry. Harry didn't have any "freight" on him, but he did have his Collie credit card—a three-foot piece of hose and a gas can. You could always get some petrol with that card.

As he approached the white Land Rover, Eggers smiled. He hadn't had to buy any gas in something like forever and tonight would be no exception. Sneaking up to the vehicle, he crouched down beside it and popped off the gas cap. Quickly and quietly, he fed the hose down into the car's fuel tank.

Eggers blew into the hose. To his surprise he felt no resistance nor heard any bubbling. He removed the hose about halfway and blew again. Still nothing. He pushed the hose as far down into the tank as it would go. Again, nothing. He had siphoned lots of Rovers and couldn't understand the problem this time.

Maybe there isn't any petrol in the tank, he thought to himself. But there *had* to be and Eggers didn't have all night. He pulled a small flashlight from his rear pocket and switched it on. The batteries were completely dead. Not to be discouraged, he reached his hand into his front pocket and came out with his cigarette lighter.

"Always pays to have a backup plan," he whispered to himself.

Now I don't know about you, but I think I was about five years old when I learned in school that it's not the fuel that ignites—it's the fumes. Apparently, Eggers had skipped school that day, but he was about to learn this on his own. Eggers lit his lighter.

There *was* fuel in the tank after all. The ensuing explosion blew him ten feet back, removing all traces of hair from his face and head, and leaving some pretty serious second-degree burns on his hands and arms.

Oh yeah, he was arrested, too!

That's a Spiceeeeeey "Meatball"!

35

(Italy)

A group of American college students on an archeological summer study program in Italy were having the time of their lives. During the day they dug and sifted through the fine Tuscan soil, uncovering Roman relics; at night they collapsed exhausted under the stars. Some evenings, though, they visited a restaurant in a nearby village to enjoy sumptuous seven-course dinners of pasta, fish, chicken, beef, and, of course, wine.

On one such evening, while the college kids were safely settled at Mama Dominici's restaurant, a drifter wandered into their dig. He helped himself to food, CD players, radios, and clothes, packed everything into a stolen backpack, and made off into the night. Actually, he stumbled into the night, falling several times in the moonless evening before giving up and deciding to wait for daylight.

The college kids returned to their camp too tired and tipsy to notice that they had been robbed; they all just crawled into their sleeping bags and started snoring. But the next morning one of the boys went for his toothbrush and realized his whole backpack was missing. He woke up his friends, and they were making an inventory of missing items when they heard a series of blood-curdling screams from nearby in the woods. They seemed to be coming from an animal in pain, and they would not stop.

The howling came closer and closer. Then they saw him. The drifter was stumbling into trees and bushes, clutching his throat, and screaming while flames shot out of his mouth! Yep, his mouth was on fire. He ran blindly into camp, collapsed to his knees, and plunged his whole head into the water bucket. His screams gurgled to a stop. Then he jerked his head up, gasped for air, and spat before plunging his head back under.

While some of the students attended to the fire-breathing drifter, two of the boys retraced his steps. Within moments they found the stolen backpack with the missing items. Lying together on the ground were a toothbrush, a pack of cigarettes, a toothpaste-like tube, and a lighter. When one boy picked up the tube, he solved the mystery.

Back in camp, they told the others what they assumed

Yep, his mouth was on fire.

had happened. The drifter had awakened and rummaged through the backpack to find a toothbrush and what he thought was toothpaste. The tube actually contained Liquid Fire, a flammable paste used to start campfires. After giving his teeth a good brushing with it, the drifter had then decided to have his first smoke of the day—with dramatic and incendiary results.

Three Strikes, and They're Out

(Canada)

Constable Tim Schewe of the Royal Canadian Mounted Police received a call one night from a small grocery store on the Alaska Highway. The store's owner reported that a break-in had occurred during the night and that more than twenty cartons of low-tar cigarettes were missing, as well as seventy-two Jerky Jim's Beef Jerkies and two cases of Hudepohl Beer.

This being Canada in November, it was a simple matter to follow footprints in the new snow to a trailer park fifty feet away. Tim asked the gentleman who answered the knock if he knew anything about the break-in at the grocery.

"No, sir; officer, sir. I don't know anything about a break-in!" The man was almost screaming. *"I've been here with my friends all night!"* At first, Tim thought he

hadn't put in his hearing aid. But while this guy was very audibly denying any knowledge of the crime, he was also pointing meaningfully down the hallway.

"In fact, my friends are still sleeping!"

Tim followed the man's gestures to a bedroom where a man lay snoring. Scattered around the bed were cartons of low-tar cigarettes, Jerky Jim wrappers, and crushed Hudepohl cans. Tim started toward the sleeping man, but his tour guide grabbed his elbow and pointed toward the closet. Sensing danger, Tim leveled his gun at the closet door.

"Come out of the closet very slowly with your hands on top of your head," he commanded.

Another gentleman stepped out of the closet, and Tim arrested both the sleeper and the closet dweller.

Back at the station, Tim just had to run a warrant check on the guy who had fingered his two sleeping friends— just to make sure that he was kosher. *Bingo!* Tim returned to the trailer park to apprehend the overly helpful citizen on an outstanding warrant for grand theft auto. Tim was three for three in the space of an hour, and he recovered fifty-four of the seventy-two Jerky Jims!

No, Honest!

(America)

An undercover officer infiltrating a California high school had been busy becoming cool enough to do business with the local schoolyard dealers. He knew he had it made the day a certain young man eased down beside him in the cafeteria.

"I heard you were looking for some dope."

"You heard right. What do you have?"

But the young man was suspicious. "You aren't a narc, are you?"

How many times had the young narc heard this question? For a change, he thought he'd try the truth.

"I sure am. I just finished with the police academy, and the drug task force asked me to come here."

The kid stared intently. Then he burst out laughing as he reached into his pocket for something to sell the truth-ful—but still undercover—officer, who had just told the nerd his departmental history.

Some dummies just never believe the truth.

Set Your Goals High

(Hong Kong)

Six young men attending college in Saskatoon were deeply envious of a wealthy classmate from Hong Kong. They were in awe of his possessions and resented his carefree attitude. He really was set for life; his parents would give him anything he wanted.

Boing! That's when the brilliant idea hit them. They would kidnap their wealthy Asian friend and hold him for ransom.

Their plan worked brilliantly. They waited until their classmate returned home on summer break and snatched him off a Hong Kong street. Who would suspect Canadian kidnappers in Hong Kong? Before he knew what hit him, the victim was whisked away to the airport, flown back to Canada, and shuttled across town to an apartment rented just for the occasion. Then he was forced to make the ransom call to his own mother.

What could he do but obey? The young man told his mom that he had been kidnapped and that his abductors were demanding a whopping fifteen thousand dollars. He told her the terms they demanded. He also told her where he was, who was holding him, and that she needed to call the Royal Canadian Mounted Police. But his kidnappers never knew about these additional instructions until much later because their prisoner was speaking to his mother in Cantonese.

They didn't understand a word, in fact, until the Mounties showed up and said, *"Freeze!"*

Flip-Flop Cop

(Australia)

A constable in Queensland broke a case wide open with an unusual investigative technique. It all started when the officer responded to a silent alarm from a small business. Someone had broken in, and several computers were missing.

While he was writing up his report, the officer noticed a pair of rubber flip-flops, or thongs, lying in one corner. The owner of the business said he had never seen them before, so the officer took them back to the station as evidence. Call it a hunch.

Later that evening at the station, the officer was doing his paperwork when three men were hauled in on a motor vehicle offense. Our deputy noticed that one of the men was not wearing shoes. Playing his hunch, the officer picked up the rubber thongs and nonchalantly dropped them to the floor as he passed the area where the suspects were being booked. As the officer continued on around the counter, the barefoot man walked over to the flip-flops, slipped them on, and walked back to his place.

"Those flip-flops belong to you?" the officer asked casually.

"Yeah, they're mine," the barefoot bungler replied. "I couldn't figure out where I'd left them. Thank you."

The officer couldn't hold back a smile. A minute before, he really hadn't had much chance of solving the computer-theft crime. Now he had a confession, the evidence to convict, and the three suspects in custody, all without leaving the station. "Oh, no," he told the casual criminal. "Thank *you!*"

Halle's Bomb-It

(Germany)

A nefarious duo in the town of Halle hatched a heinous plot that entailed sending a letter to a store owner, and threatening to bomb his grocery store. They would then go into the supermarket, pick up a quart of milk and some ham, and inconspicuously leave a small bomb on a shelf. Once outside, they would make a call and demand payment from one of the store managers, threatening to blow up the store.

They got the bomb planted all right. But things started to go awry when they called to voice their demands. The first two managers they talked to thought the bomb was a hoax and refused to pay. Their first two bombs were duds and never even fizzed. The third manager did pay off, but then the bomb went off by accident.

No one was injured, but it did damage several rows of canned yams.

This was the perfect time, of course, for our brilliant bombers to leave town. They had their money, and police were already swarming the crime scene, searching for clues, dusting for prints, and lab-testing every shred of evidence. Someone was sure to find something soon.

Did they leave? Such a sensible strategy was apparently more than their dumb criminal minds could even begin to fathom.

In the middle of the investigation, a traffic cop passing by the supermarket happened to come upon a parked car with two men asleep in it. Looking closer, he realized they were passed-out drunk. The backseat of their unlocked car was crammed with clothes, papers, and miscellaneous junk, which the suspicious officer rummaged through while they slept. Within moments he had unearthed originals of all the extortion letters, the cell phone used to make the calls, and a bag of loot.

"It was like an extortion office on wheels," he said.

Oh yes, he finally did awaken the suspects and inform them that their goose was, in fact, cooked.

Looking closer, he realized they were passed-out drunk.

41 Jag Drag

(America)

On the beautiful islands of Hawaii, it's not hard to believe that you are in paradise. The combination of perfect weather, the world's most beautiful beaches, and friendly people bearing fruit and frozen daiquiris can make for a most satisfying experience. But there are some who must drive an expensive convertible through paradise to be truly satisfied. Our next dumb criminal is just such a man.

He was driving a Jaguar XK8 two-door convertible with the top down in the brilliant Hawaiian sunshine. If car commercials are a vision of the afterlife, then this man was already in heaven. He interrupted his heavenly cruise, however, for a stop in a public park. There he met a gentleman who couldn't help but admire the beautiful automobile, which at the time was worth well over seventy thousand dollars.

"I'll sell it to you for five thousand dollars," said the driver, grinning at his dumbfounded new friend.

"You're kidding, but . . ." The prospective buyer was stunned, to say the least.

"But you've got to get the cash in the next hour," the driver added. "Can you do it? This is the car of a lifetime."

"Yeah . . . uh, can you meet me at the bank in Kapiolani?"

"In one hour. Be there with the cash, and the car is yours."

Exactly one hour later, the Jaguar jerk was arrested for grand theft auto at the Kapiolani bank. It turns out the Jaguar had been stolen the day before on a test drive from a Honolulu car dealership. It also turns out that the stranger in the park happened to be an employee of the very same dealership. He called the police as soon as he left the park, and Honolulu's finest did the rest.

How well do you know the dumb criminal mind?

While we were taping another episode of *America's Dumbest Criminals,* the person we hired to play a drug dealer didn't show up on the set that day because . . .

A. . . . he was waiting for a call back from *Baywatch*.

B. . . . someone had stolen his car.

C. . . . he was doing missionary work.

D. . . . he had been jailed for possession of drugs.

The correct answer is D. True story: The guy had been popped with twenty pounds of Wacky Tobacky the day before the shoot! How's that for typecasting?

The Big-Bag Theory

(Thailand)

Ang Lieu Khang was a busboy at Bangkok's Garden of Ecstasy restaurant which catered to the wealthiest clientele. On a good night, the manager might deposit the equivalent of ten thousand dollars in the night depository of the bank only two blocks away. At closing, the manager would transfer the money in a plain brown paper bag. Khang had watched the manager leave many times, and each time he thought to himself how easy it would be to rob his boss.

One night the chef was in a particularly foul mood and he took it all out on Khang. This was nothing new, but this night he humiliated the young man in front of his coworkers. Something inside Khang snapped. He finished his shift without a word, and the next night he was waiting in the shadows of the alley for his revenge.

Like clockwork, the manager carried his brown paper bag full of the night's revenues out the backdoor of the restaurant, only to suddenly spin around to start yelling at the cook, who screamed right back at him from the kitchen.

Khang saw his moment and shot out of the shadows. In the cover of darkness, he snatched the bag out of the air and was gone in a split second. The manager never heard him or saw him. The grab was perfectly executed and so was Khang's getaway.

Twelve blocks away in another alley, Khang stopped to catch his breath and count the take. He panted as he opened the brown paper sack. Then he fainted dead away: no money, all fish heads. The manager had actually been doing Khang's job for him, taking out the garbage.

The grab was perfectly executed and so was Khang's getaway.

43 The United Nations of Crime

(Canada)

Philip J. Cyr works as a security officer at an amusement park in Toronto. He recalls with a few chuckles the day a man with an East Indian accent tried to gain admission to the park using another man's season's pass. The photo on the pass bore no resemblance at all to the man who was presenting it, so Cyr asked him if the pass really did belong to him. The man responded in French that he spoke no English, only French.

That posed no problem for Cyr, who is bilingual in French and English. Cyr repeated his question in impeccable French. The visitor looked at Cyr, stunned. Then, his bluff called, he managed a laugh. "Did I say French?" he said, now speaking Spanish. "I meant Spanish. I only speak Spanish."

Go figure.

Okay, so here's a man who said, in French, that he spoke only French and then said, in Spanish, that he spoke only Spanish. The look on his face quickly changed from humor to horror when Cyr asked him the same question for a third time, this time in Spanish. It seems that Cyr had also taken two years of high school Spanish.

Now the guy was so angry with Cyr that he began to curse—in English. Cyr told the poor guy that he was being too hard on himself.

"Your English is quite good, really."

The look the frustrated visitor gave him would have communicated clearly in *any* language.

Just His Bad Puck

(England)

"Wear a mask," is a basic rule of crime. A dumb criminal should remember to check that his or her mask has eyeholes. A really dumb criminal should also make sure that the eyeholes are in the right place.

Such was *not* the case at a hold-up in a small village in Kent. Dumb criminal Mack Brown had a mask, all right. And it did have eyeholes. Unfortunately for him, the eyeholes had been cut an inch to the left and a half-inch below the actual eyes in his head. Lacking the foresight to try on his mask ahead of time, Mack didn't realize he was in the dark until he started to enter the store he was about to rob.

Stepping blindly through the door, Mack fumbled with one hand to line up his eyeholes while he searched for his knife with the other. Seeing all this, the shop owner

He picked up his hockey stick and smacked Mack right in the ear with a slapshot.

didn't wait for explanations. He picked up his hockey stick and smacked Mack right in the ear with a slapshot that sent Mack skittering across the floor into the waiting hands of a constable, who happened to be shopping in the store at the time.

Mack was charged with attempted armed robbery and received four years. The shop owner was charged with high sticking and received two minutes in the penalty box.

Wishful Thinking

45

(Italy)

It was the late 1950s, and Emilio Puccini was a rookie on patrol in Rome during the wee hours of the morning. The city was very still and beautiful at this hour, the dark, quiet time just after the late-night revelers had turned in and just before the fish market came to life. It was usually so quiet during Puccini's watch that he could hear a drunk mumble a couple of blocks away. One night, however, he was startled to hear somebody suddenly screaming in English.

"I wish . . . I wish . . . I had some money!" The voice was clearly that of a young man, coming from the direction of the famous Trevi Fountain. Puccini heard a big splash as he trotted toward the voice. He arrived just in time to see the young man surface with his two hands filled with coins.

"Thank you. But . . . but . . . I wish I had more money!"

Apparently oblivious to his surroundings, the inebriated young man shoved the coins into his pockets and submerged again to gather up more from the bottom of the fountain. Puccini watched him dive for money several times before he hauled the dripping, sloshing lad to the sidewalk. When Puccini rattled off several terse comments in Italian, the young man gave Puccini a very puzzled look, then grabbed a handful of coins from his pocket and threw them back into the fountain while he screamed, *"I wish I spoke Italian!"*

It seems he had simply enjoyed too much wine and had run out of money. When the officer described the charities the coins were intended for, the young man quickly returned his pounds of loot. The loony part, he gets to keep.

On a Kaiser Roll

46

(Germany)

Heinrich Wehrman of Bonn had one too many steins of the ol' meister brau that night. He'd arrived at the bar around seven that evening and had been drinking heavily ever since. It was now well after midnight, and the usually short drive home was taking forever.

Wehrman was having trouble keeping his eyes open and everything appeared blurry. He closed his eyes often and rubbed them, hoping to clear his vision. Suddenly, he felt the front wheels of his vehicle veer to the left. He opened his eyes quickly, but it was too late. He pulled hard to the right to avoid the three pedestrians now directly in his path, but there wasn't time. He heard screams and saw the look of sheer terror on their faces as he lost consciousness.

At Wehrman's trial, the judge was reluctant to send the crippled man to jail, but justice must be served.

"Mr. Wehrman, you've been found guilty of driving while intoxicated. You were so drunk that you struck three people with your vehicle. You were very lucky someone wasn't killed. Be that as it may, I have no choice but to sentence you to the maximum six days in jail. And in the future, should you find yourself in a similar condition, you are hereby ordered not to drive your motorized wheelchair!"

A G-Man-Style Takedown

47

(America)

Back in 1984, Chris Thomas was an FBI agent stationed in Washington, D.C., but engaged to a young woman who lived in New York City. Whenever Thomas got a night off and his fiancée could get away, she would hop on the shuttle and come down for a Saturday evening together.

On one such evening in the spring, the young couple decided to enjoy the night air with a walk among the cherry blossoms near the Capitol mall. Everything seemed perfect . . . until the two teenagers appeared with a pistol, demanding money. Thomas was furious, especially because these two young fools had broken the spell of the evening. Without really thinking, he reached into his jacket pocket and pulled out his badge in its

125

leather holder, thrusting it in the boys' faces and screamed, *"FBI!"*

The two boys backed up a step. "It's cool, man. Everybody's cool." They never stopped stepping back as they lowered the pistol. "We didn't mean anything. We're cool." Then they ran off into the night.

Thomas and his fiancée had a good laugh and breathed a huge sigh of relief. But as soon as the boys ran off, Thomas realized he had grabbed his wallet, not his badge. While he was screaming *"FBI!"* the two boys had actually been staring at a photo of his fiancée. They must have thought he was crazy—and maybe he was. But Thomas still wasn't sorry for what he had done. In all his years of programming computers for the Bureau, he had always wanted to do that to a bad guy!

Let the Games Begin!

48

(Canada)

The World Police-Fire Games were held one summer in Calgary. The games pit different police and firefighter teams against one another in athletic and work-related events of speed, accuracy, agility, and strength. Teams from all over Canada and many other countries compete. There's no big prize except for the glory and the honor, but it is also a great time of camaraderie and what we'll loosely call "networking."

One homicide sergeant from Regina got an extra bonus for attending the games and winning a special event. He nabbed the suspect in a high-profile murder case, a man the sergeant had been after for some time. He was standing right next to him in the crowd, observing the festivities. All the cop had to do was turn, grab the guy's arm, and say, "You're under arrest."

It was the fastest homicide arrest of the games.

Flight to Freedom

(Albania)

Before the Iron Curtain came crashing down, Albania's dictatorial government had been particularly brutal and paranoid. Travel for the average citizen was unthinkable. But Ivan Ruzica had hope—hope inspired by a bootleg videotape.

Ruzica had seen a black-market copy of the American film *Iron Eagle,* in which a sixteen-year-old boy flies an F-16 fighter behind enemy lines to rescue his imprisoned father. Ruzica thought, *If this child can fly such a plane, so can Ivan.* Ruzica was probably inspired a bit by the fifth of vodka he had just knocked back.

A muddled plan formed. He stumbled out of his barracks and down to the hangar. True, Ruzica was in the Albanian air force. And yes, for the last seven and a half months, he had worked around the big MIG fighters. But

The canopy was open and Ruzian slid down into the pilot's seat.

Ruzica was the base landscaper. He was not a pilot, nor had he any training to fly.

When he sneaked up to the fighter, the sentry was at the other end of the hangar. The canopy was open and Ruzica slid down into the pilot's seat. He slipped on the helmet. He pulled the crank on the side of the cockpit and the canopy began to lower. He gave thumbs-up to his imaginary crew just like the kid in the movie. Then he reached down and hit the big red button on the right.

Ruzica was instantly hurtled into space. His face pulled back from the G forces as he shot right up toward the stars—without his plane. Ruzica had ejected from the parked plane. Unfortunately, he did not get high enough for his chute to deploy fully. After his seat hit the tarmac, the chute quietly fluttered down to cover Ruzica, sitting upright, unconscious in the pilot's seat. They found him about fifty feet from the parked plane.

Which goes to show, some people just can't handle ejection.

Fashion Victim

(Australia)

It seems there was a young man in Melbourne who had a real obsession with the latest fashions. Whatever color was in, whatever fashion was hot at the moment, he *had* to have it. Unfortunately, this man's income couldn't keep pace with his fashion addiction, so he began to add to his wardrobe from outdoor clotheslines all over town. Usually it would be several days before the owner noticed a garment missing, if he ever noticed at all.

By all appearances, our fashion-plate perpetrator had found his ticket to Mr. Blackwell's Best-Dressed List on the cheap. But then he got careless. En route to the local cinema one day, he spotted a snazzy dark-blue shirt hanging on his neighbor's clothesline. It was a beautiful and very expensive shirt—irresistible to our dumb criminal. He slipped it right off the line and onto his back, then continued his walk to the movies wearing his new "off the rack" fashion statement.

Unfortunately for him, his neighbor was standing right in front of him in line at the cinema, buying a ticket with the girlfriend who had given him the shirt.

"Isn't that the shirt I gave you last week?" she quietly asked her boyfriend.

"If it's not, it's one just like it."

So the girlfriend turned and walked over to the man.

"I love your shirt," she told the unsuspecting loser, batting her eyes. "Where did you get it? I'd love to buy one just like it for my boyfriend."

The dumb criminal beamed. He was right: Clothes *do* make the man. "Oh, one of the shops downtown, I forget."

Another bat of the eyes. "May I see the label?"

Our rummage-sale Romeo couldn't resist a chance to show off, so he turned around and let her check inside his collar. Yep, there was her boyfriend's name, "Rodney," sewn in below the designer label.

"Wow, it's a designer label. This must have been very expensive, Rodney." She winked at her boyfriend as the dumb clotheshorse corrected her.

"*My* name's not Rodney, it's Frank."

Time for the real Rodney to step in.

"*My* name is Rodney. Remember me? I live next door to you, and that's my favorite shirt you're wearing."

"I paid good money for this shirt," the dummy protested, but the girlfriend protested louder and smarter.

"No, I paid good money for that shirt, and I sewed Rodney's name in the collar."

The jig was up. The police found several other "Rodneys" in Frank's closet, not to mention a couple of "Bobs," one or two "Toms," and a number of "Geoffs."

Now Frank just has the one suit, but it is monogrammed with his very own prison number.

They Didn't Get Clean Away

(Thailand)

Police in the Thai province of Ayutthaya had for some time been stumped by a rash of break-ins in affluent neighborhoods. Forty houses had been hit. In each case, the only clue had been a broken cement sewage tank under each house—and no hint of a suspect.

In need of a break or at least another clue, investigators were granted their wish when they were told about a free-spending group of suddenly wealthy eleven- and twelve-year-old boys. Working carefully but aggressively, police followed the gang of skinny youths to their meeting place under a bridge. From there the group split up and started out into a neighborhood that had already been victimized many times in recent months.

The cops watched as one youth slithered through an opening under the house that was no more than twenty

They found the culprit half out of the toilet hole.

inches high. About fifteen minutes later, he appeared at the front door, freshly showered and with his arms full of loot. His accomplices raced off in one direction with the loot while he strolled away in the other.

At the next house, the police moved in as soon as the point man slid under the house. Inside the house, they found the culprit half out of the toilet hole—the porcelain opening that Thais squat over instead of using a standard toilet bowl.

It seems our potty robber would break into the sewage tank, slide through the waste, and come out head first through the toilet and into the house. After a quick shower, the tiny thief would scoop up all the valuables and, in a matter of minutes, meet his friends at the front door.

But not anymore. Once caught, these kids were literally and figuratively in deep doo-doo.

Jean-Claude "Damn Van"

52

(France)

It had been raining for a week straight and Jean-Claude Bouchet was glad of it. Bouchet was a thief and he loved this time of the year in Paris. People stayed indoors to keep dry, windows were more difficult to see out of, and any inadvertent fingerprints left behind were washed away by the steady rainfall.

Ah, April in Paris.

Breaking into cars and trucks was Bouchet's specialty. He could case a vehicle, quietly pop out a window, and be gone with the contents in less than thirty seconds. The last week had been a treasure trove of cameras, purses, wallets, and even a bass fiddle.

From the darkness of the alley, he studied the white van parked directly across the street as he strolled toward it. Without breaking stride, he casually placed his hand on the hood of the van as he stepped up on the curb. The engine was cold, meaning it had been parked for a good while, and the windows were darkly tinted. This usually meant there was something in there to hide.

This wasn't the safest of neighborhoods, and whoever parked here either didn't know it or had mechanical trouble. *They'll be in for a surprise when they get back,* he chuckled to himself as he slipped the pry bar from his pant leg via his waist.

Walking to the rear of the van, he gave a quick look around and tried the handle. Locked. Next he slid the bar into the door seams beside the lock and pulled sharply. The metal bent and the pry bar popped out. He dug in a little deeper with the edge and gave a strong grunt and, suddenly, *pow*! The door burst open with such force that it knocked him to the pavement. He was instantly set upon by no fewer than four Paris police officers, handcuffed, and placed under arrest.

Bouchet had just broken into a police surveillance van. The French speak a different language, but if you mention *idiot,* people understand what you mean. *Au revoir.*

Mission Improbable

(Canada)

Justice Spyros D. Loukidelis of Sudbury recounts a tale of two buffoons from British Columbia who pulled into a strip mall to rob a small branch bank. They were as well rehearsed and well choreographed as a movie cast, but the end effect was more Marx Brothers than *Mission Impossible.*

It began smoothly enough. The black sedan slid silently along the curb and eased to a stop. Two darkly clad figures slithered out, crouched behind the car, and snapped out two black ski masks. Simultaneously, they slid the masks over their heads and stood.

That's when they realized they had both put their masks on backward.

Blindly, they knelt and spun their masks around, then each drew a pistol with a silencer. Darting single file behind the car, they leaped up onto the sidewalk, flattening themselves against the wall as they scanned the area with their guns. The leader whipped open the door, and they were inside.

They squeezed off a round into the ceiling to maximize the element of surprise, but no one even turned to look at them. They looked puzzled for a split second, then both mouthed the word *silencers.* So the leader screamed, *"Freeze! This is a bank robbery!"*

An elderly woman behind the counter felt obliged to respond, "No, it's not."

The two men spun to face her. "What?"

"This would be a Singer Sewing Center robbery," she explained. "If you were two doors down, now that would be a bank robbery."

Cursing, the two men darted out the door and made their way commando-style down the sidewalk and into the bank. Breathing hard, they demanded, "We want all the money! *Now*!"

The single teller on duty immediately started to empty the money from her drawer.

"Put it in the bag!" the leader demanded.

The teller looked perplexed. "What bag?"

"Do you have the bag?" the lead gunman asked his partner.

The guy had to set his gun down to check all his pockets. "It must've fallen out when I pulled out my mask."

His partner sighed. "Do you have a bag, ma'am?"

The teller looked through several cabinets to find a bag. Then she made a great show of stuffing in fistfuls of money, mainly smaller bills. Quite tense by now, the less-than-dynamic duo grabbed the borrowed bag, bolted from the bank, and sprinted to their car. Now, it was the lead gunman's turn to look through his pockets.

"Wait," he said, "I'll be right back." His partner just stared as he jumped out and raced back into the bank. He never noticed that the teller was on the phone to the police. He was too intent on grabbing the car keys off the counter and hurrying back to the car where his partner waited. Finally, they got the car started and pulled away—just in time to be cut off on all sides by squad cars.

Serves You Right

(America)

It was about three in the morning when a Seattle police officer responded to a call from a man who was staying in his motor home outside a friend's house. The man had been awakened by a peculiar noise outside and he had used his cell phone to call police.

The officer found the evidence fairly self-explanatory. Someone had tried to siphon gas from the trailer with a garden hose, which still dangled from the open tank. Coming closer, however, the officer realized the criminal's mistake: The hose was dangling from the sewage tank instead of the gas tank. A little trail of untreated sewage led the officer to a nearby parked car and the teenaged culprit, who was still quite ill.

Easy Come, Easy Go

(Germany)

A trio of troublesome fellows in Hamburg were playing cards one night. Hand after hand, they all folded. None of them had a bit of luck. Frustrated by the dullness of their game, they finally decided to up the stakes and rob a large grocery store around the corner. After a few beers, it all seemed so simple. *We wear masks and pull our guns, they hand us money, and it's over.*

It did turn out to be very simple. They pulled off the robbery exactly as planned and got away with twenty-three hundred deutsche marks. (It helped that the host had an automatic weapon in the closet.) Now the intrepid trio decided to celebrate. They parked their car on a seedy side of town near the red-light district and started out on foot to find some female companionship.

While these stooges were partying and spending all their stolen money, however, a passing policeman happened to notice the automatic weapon lying in plain view in their car's back seat. He also noticed that they were illegally parked. He called to have the car towed away.

When the tired threesome finally came straggling back to where they had parked, they found themselves staring at an empty curb. They finally figured out that their getaway car had been towed, so they did what any good citizen would do—they cussed a little and then called to find out where they could pick up their vehicle.

Sure enough, the police had their car. They had the gun, which a witness had already identified from the robbery. The police also had the masks used in the robbery, which had been left in the car as well.

The police had everything connected with the robbery, in fact, except the stolen money and the criminals themselves. That's what Moe, Larry, and Curly provided when they showed up for their car—with twenty-one hundred deutsche marks still wadded up in their pockets.

The Three Un-Wise Men

(Syria)

Justice can be swift in the villages of Syria. The great deterrent to crime is much like our Old West. The fact is, if you're caught red-handed, you stand a very good chance of losing that hand or having your neck stretched, depending on the mood of the local populace.

And just like our Old West, there are always young men willing to take the chance rather than work for a living.

Gamal, Mustafa, and Hassan were out for themselves and themselves only. They were the first generation of Syrians to have grown up exposed to western television and movies. The three amigos could quote the old Hollywood westerns by heart. They were now the "Younger Brothers," a modern-day reincarnation of three of the blood-thirstiest, meanest, bank-robbingest bad guys the West had ever seen. Or so they thought.

The three rifles were easy to get: Almost everyone in the countryside hunts, and those who don't are armed anyway. They made their getaway from their parents' house at night without a note or a word. Silently, they left the village, two on foot and the third on a burro. They traveled for an hour before they set up their hideout. It was a desert region and the boys had a tent up in no time.

Gamal had the master plan. They were going to rob the "stage," a bank armored car, at 8:00 A.M. They had their bandannas ready, guns, and plenty of ammo. By morning, they would be legends.

Hassan was assigned sentry duty first. At night in the desert, you think you can see much farther than you actually can. In the blue light of a star-filled sky, the desert can play tricks on the eye. Hassan was on edge. When a lizard darted across the desert twenty feet away, the trigger-happy youth instinctively popped off a round. Hassan stared in disbelief. He had destroyed the lizard.

Gamal and Mustafa bolted out of the tent with their rifles ready.

"Nothing but a lizard," Hassan drawled slowly in his best Clint Eastwood as he pointed at what used to be a lizard. With the cool disdain of a hired gun, Hassan stuck his rifle in the sand, barrel down. Mustafa and Gamal grunted and went back to sleep.

Hassan's confidence was pumped now that he had

tasted bloodshed. He scanned the horizon, hoping for another chance to fire the gun. Then there it was. *Was it a man's silhouette or just a cloud's moon shadow?* Was Hassan seeing things? Finally, the shape came over a rise fifty feet from Hassan. It was a man, a big man.

Hassan leapt to his feet. Like Chuck Connors on *The Rifleman,* he whipped his gun out of the sand, swung it up to his shoulder, and fired at the silhouette. The gun gave a muffled blast, spitting sand and a bullet about fifteen feet. The silhouette rushed up as Hassan screamed. The next thing he knew, his gun was wrenched from his hands and the man was now cuffing Hassan on the ears just the way his father did when he was being punished.

Yikes, this *was* his father, but the punishment was just beginning. Hassan's dad disarmed the Younger Brothers single-handedly.

DUMB CRIMINALS' TOP-10 LIST

The World's Top Ten Alibis and Excuses

Almost every law enforcement officer we've met the world over has a personal list of outrageous alibis and excuses he or she has been fed by dumb criminals. Here is a list of our own favorites:

10. "They're not my pants!" (This three-hundred-pound dumb criminal had been caught with a gun in his back pants' pocket. When asked whose pants they were, the guy pointed to his ninety-pound girlfriend. "She used to be much larger," he explained. The policeman then had to intervene to save the man from his petite but outraged paramour.)

9. "I couldn't have robbed that house because at that time I was robbing the house a block and a half from there."

8. "I know I was speeding, but this is a Mercedes; it's the safest car in the world."

7. "I had to steal the car to get to court."

6. "Someone has been spreading my fingerprints all over town."

5. "I didn't steal it. It was already stolen." (This particular dumb criminal watched another crook steal the car, rip out the stereo, and run. So he went ahead and hot-wired the car for his own use. "It was like the laws of salvage," he told officers. "It was abandoned.")

4. "I wasn't really speeding. I just washed my car, and I was blowing it dry."

3. "No one could identify me in that stolen car because I had on a ballcap and the car's windows were tinted."

2. "I went to McDonald's with my friend from the guest house and then chipped a few golf balls in the dark. Then I left town right after the crime."

1. "I didn't do no Armstrong robbery, and I'll blow in a polygram to prove it!" (This brilliant comment came from a less-than-educated criminal being accused of a strong-arm robbery.)

 # An Irish Tale

(Ireland)

Now, mind you, this is an unconfirmed bit of what might be blarney from an off-duty local officer, but we'll report it all the same because it just might be true—even if only in the Republic of Ireland.

The officer in question was making his way down a narrow road between Waterville and Kenmare when he observed a car driving erratically. In a moment he had caught up to the car and popped on his lights. One quick blast of the siren brought the car jerkily to the side of the road. The officer made note of the license plate and cautiously stepped out to approach the vehicle.

Meanwhile, the car's two occupants were discussing strategy. Both were well inebriated, but the passenger had a plan.

"Take the label off the whiskey bottle and put it on

your forehead and don't say a word," he said, "I'll do all the talking."

The driver was so gone that he obeyed immediately. The passenger disposed of the bottle, and the driver turned to face the officer with a "Bushmill's" label on his forehead. The officer inspected this spectacle for a moment, then asked with a grin, "Now, you two gentlemen wouldn't have been drinking tonight, would you?"

The passenger quickly replied with a bit of a slur, "No, sir. No indeed, sirrrrr. We were at our Alcoholics Anonymous meeting. As you can see, my friend is on the patch." Without saying a word, the driver pointed to the label on his forehead and nodded.

As we said, only in Ireland.

58 Ouch, I've Arrested Myself

(Canada)

A man was stealing sheets of plywood from a building supply company in Saskatoon during the middle of the night. One by one, he hefted the heavy, awkward sheets of wood onto his truck.

He was working for almost an hour, when he stumbled and fell. When he tried to get up, he couldn't budge.

The poor guy had fallen face-first onto the stack of plywood while holding a sheet in front of him. When he fell, he smashed his fingertips under the plywood. Now all of his weight was on top of the plywood, pushing down on his fingers.

He couldn't get his hands out because he couldn't get off the plywood. And he couldn't get off the plywood because his fingers were stuck. He lay there all night until an employee found him the next morning.

Choo-Choo Boo-Boo

(The Netherlands)

The setting was a very expensive department store in Amsterdam, filled with exotic delights for the Christmas shopping season. The time was after midnight, and nothing was moving in the dark store except for a lone dark figure in the jewelry department—an old pro at breaking and entering. Scooping up diamonds and watches with nonchalant skill, our man filled his bag and started to leave just like any tired shopper. Our man would be the first to testify that the holiday season sure was a wonderful time to shop, especially after hours, when the price is right.

Then he saw it, in the toy department—the model railroad of his youthful dreams. He couldn't resist. Using his flashlight to find the transformer, the thief lay flat out on the floor and opened up the throttle on the

Then he saw it, in the toy department—the model railroad of his youthful dreams.

big locomotive. It pulled twenty cars—passengers cars, dining cars, even a few freight cars filled with presents and a bright red caboose!

Ol' Casey Jones was having the time of his life when two strong hands lifted him right up off the floor. Although the thief had set off a silent alarm, he had been too engrossed in his play even to hear the police arrive!

60 Kick Me, Wash Me, Pay Me

(America)

Keeping your car cold and dirty can pay off! That's what a New Hampshire man found out when his parked automobile was hit by a passing motorist who decided to keep right on going. The man's car was caked with mud and frost, which allowed the hit-and-run vehicle to leave a perfect imprint of its license tag. The officers were amazed when every bit of information appeared, backward but perfectly legible on the victim's bumper.

Go Ahead, You Can Cry for Me, Argentina.

(Argentina)

The teller at a major Argentina bank had been robbed on two occasions in her thirteen years there.

All sorts of things fly through the mind at moments like that. Your life flashes before your eyes. Thoughts of loved ones, unfinished business, even your own funeral are not unusual in a victim's account of a crime. But this robbery was different.

Theresa was once again being held at gunpoint, but she was not afraid. The only thing that she could think, the one thought that filled her mind was *This is my boss*!

Maybe it was the suit the robber wore, just like the one that Mr. Rodriguez had worn to work that morning. Perhaps it was the fact that the robber had called Theresa by her first name yet she wore a nametag that read "Mrs. Garcia." Or maybe, just maybe, it was the fact that the robber stuttered when he demanded the money, just like Mr. Rodriguez always did when he got nervous or stressed out. And true, Mr. Rodriguez had been acting very strangely when he left for lunch just ten minutes earlier.

Theresa did not have to speak or confront her boss though. The security guard Mr. Rodriguez himself had hired brought him down with a thud.

It seems Mr. Rodriguez was embezzling and, in his desperation, he thought he could make a withdrawal at lunch and a deposit in the afternoon at his own bank branch!

The No-Tell Motel Telltale Tale

62

(Australia)

A young man entered the lobby of a motel in Brisbane. He seemed nervous and ill-at-ease, until he saw the clerk behind the counter. She was a fetching young woman. When she smiled, he melted.

"May I help you, sir?" Her voice was even lovelier than her deep blue eyes, in which he was obviously lost.

"Sir?"

"Oh, uh, yes. How much are your rooms?"

She politely gave him a rate card and explained what was available for the evening.

"Oh, no. I have a friend coming in about a week. It's for him. Would you go out with me?" He had forgotten why he had come to the motel in the first place. She declined his sudden offer but, undeterred, he wrote down

159

his name and number and told her to call if she changed her mind.

About a week later the same lovely young woman was on duty when a man in a ski mask burst into the lobby and demanded all the money in a deep, gruff voice. She frantically gathered up all the money and shoved it across the counter.

The bad guy was staring at her as he took the money. In a much higher, much more pleasant voice, he said "Thank you," and ran out. The voice seemed familiar. It reminded the clerk of the would-be suitor who had come by the week before, so she gave the police the name and phone number she had been given.

The police went to check him out. There he was, with all the money and a piece of paper on which he had written down the clerk's name and the motel's phone number. Case closed.

Will the Next Dumb Criminal Sign In, Please?

(England)

A Taunton, Somerset, shop allowed a certain citizens' group to leave a petition on the shop's front counter, primarily because the shop owner agreed with the group's agenda.

Some customers signed, others did not. Then one afternoon a pair of young men poking around inside the shop asked about the petition. A shop assistant explained that the petition sought better policing for Taunton. The two civic-minded citizens signed immediately. Then they held up the clerk at knifepoint.

When the police took the clerk's statement, they dismissed the petition names as phonies. One detective, however, stubbornly believed in the premise of never overestimating the power of the criminal mind. On a whim, he decided to stop by the address that the two young men had left on the petition.

Sure enough, they were home, and so was the stolen money. These young dumb criminals got what they asked for—better policing!

The Accent Is on You

(Spain)

Back in 1967, on the Spanish island of Allegoro, only one small store sold newspapers—the island weekly and a few other papers that arrived via a boat from the mainland. This scarcity of news was not a problem for most island residents, who weren't that interested in mainland goings-on. But a big, blond Russian who had somehow ended up on Allegoro was very interested in the state of politics in Eastern Europe. The English-language *International Herald Tribune* was the only paper in Allegoro he could read. So every week after his arrival on Allegoro he would trek to the tiny shop for his paper.

It wasn't long before the Russian began to run out of money. There were not many odd jobs on the island, and the Russian's trade (he had been a lumberjack in Russia) was not in demand. He begged the fishermen for work, but he knew nothing about the sea and was prone to seasickness besides. Everyone wondered what he would do.

And then, one balmy afternoon, the island store was robbed. The shopkeeper's young daughter was working there alone when a masked gunman came in and demanded all the money. She gave it over, and the man fled.

It was by far the biggest crime in Allegoro history. It was also the easiest to solve. For not only had the robber demanded the money in the unmistakable Russian accent of a visiting seasick lumberjack; he had also demanded a copy of the *International Herald Tribune*. Not to mention that he was the only Russian on the island, the only Eastern European, the only man at least six feet, five inches tall, and the only blond male.

They found him with all of the money, still reading the paper.

With One Hand Tied Behind My Back

(Germany)

In Hamburg, there is a small bank branch office that opens for business only three days a week. Locals don't have to fight the crowded roads to the city and the teller knows everyone by name. Almost everyone, that is.

One Friday afternoon a stranger walked in. The teller greeted him cheerfully, but the stranger didn't reply. Looking around to make sure no one else was in the bank, the stranger pulled a gun.

"This is a robbery. Give me all the money."

The robber grabbed the cash and tied the teller to a rolling chair. Oh, and he tied just one of her hands. After he left, she rolled over to a phone, reported the robbery, and untied herself with her free hand.

She literally thwarted his robbery with one hand tied behind her back.

Right Is Right

(America)

An especially brilliant criminal in a small Iowa town decided to rob a bank. He planned carefully, executed his plan, and got away with the money. But he was arrested the next day at a motel near the state line, only twenty or thirty miles away.

When asked why he had stopped so close to the scene of the crime, he explained that he was on parole and couldn't cross the state line without permission from his parole officer.

Oh.

A Clean Getaway

(Austria)

Something just wasn't right on the night train from Vienna to Brindisi, Italy. The conductor had been feeling that way ever since the train made its midnight stop. He had moved through the cars as usual to punch tickets. The sleeping passengers had left their tickets out so he wouldn't have to wake them. He was sure he had punched a ticket for every passenger . . . or had he?

Shaking his head, the conductor made his way back through the cars, even stopping to check the bathrooms. When he pounded on one bathroom door, an older woman's voice cried out for him to be patient. No surprise there. He moved on.

After the train made its next stop, our conscientious conductor repeated his rounds. This time, he found, a different bathroom was occupied—and the one that the woman had been in seemed unusually clean for this stage of the journey.

The train stopped again at around four in the morning, and the conductor still had the feeling that something was wrong. Making his rounds a third time, he found yet another bathroom occupied, the previously occupied bathroom beautifully clean . . . and now the little light bulb went on over his head.

Returning to the now-occupied bathroom, he rapped on the door and heard a gruff male voice telling him to "Try the next car." He waited a few moments and knocked again lightly. This time a *woman's* voice called out, *"une momento."* After a third knock, he heard an *old man's* voice protesting. Aha! The conductor's master key quickly revealed a teenager who had a talent for accents.

It turned out that the young man had been moving from bathroom to bathroom to avoid buying a ticket. Feeling guilty and bored, however, he had cleaned while he rode. In fact, he had done such a good job on the toilets and sinks that the conductor decided not to call the *carbineri*. Instead, he instructed the hygienic stowaway to finish latrine duty throughout the train.

Coming Attractions

68

(Canada)

A small drugstore in southern British Columbia prided itself on providing personal service. The pharmacist knew all his customers by name and was familiar with their medical histories. So he wasn't surprised when a local troublemaker demanded that he fill an outdated prescription. He was well aware of Reggie's substance-abuse problem. What did surprise him, however, was Reggie's promise to return in half an hour to rob the drugstore.

The pharmacist alerted the local police, who scratched their heads, unable to remember another case in which a robber gave advance notice. Just in case, they stopped by to see if Reggie would keep his word.

Sure enough, Reggie arrived with a hunting knife, demanding money and drugs. A Mountie quickly intervened to disarm Reggie, who, as the pharmacist sympathetically pointed out, had been two minutes late to his own robbery.

Ash Kicker

(England)

Howard Rutledge was in shock. He had returned home that morning to his Tudor-style house in Staffordshire to find a fleet of fire trucks and several policemen poking through the charred rubble of what used to be his house. The fire had consumed everything. Fortunately, he had just renewed his homeowner's insurance policy.

As he stared in stunned disbelief, a policeman approached him.

"Morning, sir." the officer said softly. "This must be your house."

"Was my house," Rutledge replied. "I was out of town. Any idea how the fire started?"

"Not at this time, although it appears to have begun in the kitchen. I'll need some information from you, sir. Meanwhile, go ahead if you'd care to look about for a bit."

Rutledge began systematically sifting through the debris. While walking through the still-smoldering ashes, he spotted what he'd been looking for. A smile came to his face. All was not lost. Though thoroughly blackened, the fire-proof valuables box had survived the raging fire. Had the contents? He glanced left and right. With the toe of his shoe he slowly lifted the corner of the box from the ashes. He bent down and took a key from his pocket. Another glance around and he quickly unlocked it. Bingo! The several thousand pounds had survived intact, as well as some personal papers and the eight ounces of pure heroin still in its asbestos sleeves. He was still smiling when he heard the constable clear his throat.

"Ahem."

"Yes?" Rutledge squeaked, slamming the lid shut.

"Forgive the pun, sir, but if that's what I think it is, your ash is mine!"

It was, and it was, and he was sentenced to fifteen years in prison.

The fire-proof valuables box had survived the raging fire.

70 Never Go to Court without It

(Colombia)

The young man faced the judge's bench with head hung low. He had come to Cartagena to face trial for possession of a controlled substance—an ounce of marijuana. Because it was a first offense, however, the judge was lenient and gave him a suspended sentence.

The young man sighed with relief . . . until the judge added that he would serve thirty days in jail just to see what happened to convicted drug users. The young man was led away. Thirty minutes later he was back again to explain the two ounces of cocaine jailers had found taped under his arm. His plan to make a delivery as soon as the judge let him off would now have to be put on indefinite hold.

Attack of the Fifty-Foot Idiot

(America)

One of the country's last drive-in theaters, this one in Washington, D.C., was the scene of one of history's worst-botched robberies.

The mishaps began when the two young thieves set out to steal a getaway car. They selected the easiest car to steal, not the best one to drive. Sure enough, it stopped dead in the road about a quarter mile from the theater.

Undeterred, the would-be criminals pushed the car off the road and walked the rest of the way to the theater. Only after several friends had waved at them on the way did they remember to pull the bandannas down over their faces. But that didn't stop the box-office clerk from calling them by name. She knew them from high school.

Determined to get on with their crime, the robbers denied who they were and stuck to their plan. One of the culprits pulled out an uninsulated pair of wire cutters to cut the phone lines, but he cut into a 220-volt electrical line instead. While he was lying senseless, his accomplice pulled a gun and demanded the box office money.

"This a joke, right?" she asked, then reached out and pulled his bandanna down. "See, I knew it was you."

Insisting that he was very serious, he set down his gun to adjust the bandanna.

Whereupon she picked up the gun and the phone and called the police—just like in the movies!

Arrest Report Fettucine

(Australia)

A police officer in Sydney had picked up a man on a warrant for several burglaries. After bringing the man back to the station for booking and questioning, she took the suspect into the interrogation room, under video surveillance, to give him the bad news:

"We've got several eyewitnesses who place you at the scene of the crimes and enough evidence to convict you three times over. It's all right here in black and white, so why don't you just confess, and maybe the magistrate will go easy on you."

"No way. I'm innocent, I tell ya."

The suspect was using Dumb Criminal Strategy Number 1: Deny, deny, deny.

There was a knock at the door, and the officer answered it. In the few seconds that her back was turned, the suspect grabbed the arrest report and shoved it into his mouth, chewing voraciously.

When the officer sat back down at the table, she looked for her notes. They weren't on the table. They weren't in her chair. They weren't under the table.

"What have you done with my notes?"

"Muffin." He was trying to say "nothing," but his mother had never taught him not to talk with his mouth full.

The video replay provided a laugh for the entire department. Our dumb criminal didn't realize that cops the world over do all their paperwork at least in triplicate. The evidence he thought he was eating was nothing but a healthy snack—low cholesterol, high fiber, and very high comedy.

The Titanic Coupe De Ville

73

(America)

Officer Will O'Diear answered a traffic accident call late one night. It seems two drunks in the southern city had gone through a stop sign and had swerved to miss a car in the intersection. They took out a fire hydrant that began spewing water under their car. Being in the condition they were in, the two drunks weren't about to exit the car anytime soon, either.

The front wheels of the car had climbed up a guy wire that supported a telephone pole. So the two drunks were facing the sky, with the car standing on its rear bumper. And they were sinking.

The broken hydrant was pouring out hundreds of gallons of water and eating away at the mud beneath the car.

The car was slowly oozing down into the sinkhole. Officer O'Diear got there just in time to help the two muddy drunks to safety, as they watched their Titanic Coupe De Ville go down for good.

Imagine explaining that to the insurance company. "No. I didn't total it. I sank it at an intersection."

Read Between the Lines

74

(Germany)

A genius in Hamburg had concocted a nifty scam. He would park alongside a motorway and take potshots at passing cars. Then he would send a note to the local government, threatening to continue the random shootings until his demands for money were met.

Instead of giving in to the extortionist's demands, however, local detectives used a simple child's trick to locate and arrest him.

The extortion letter had been written by hand on notepad paper. By gently rubbing the surface with the side of a lead pencil, they were able to detect the last thing the extortionist had written on the pad *before* the note—including, as if by magic, his name, address, and phone number.

All they had to do then was drive by and pick him up at the address he had provided them with.

But, Mom, You Said I Needed to Show Initiative!

(England)

Magistrate Pam Mills of Devonshire raised three boys of her own, so she knows mischief when she sees it. She was also very direct and strict with her boys, so it comes naturally to her to "Just say no"—even to a bungling bank robber.

It happened the morning Magistrate Mills went to the bank to deposit the proceeds from a weekend charity event. The teller counted out the pounds and pence while Mrs. Mills looked on, thrilled that the event had been so successful. She and the teller were so intent on the transaction that they barely heard a gruff voice saying, "Give me the money."

On reflex Mrs. Mills shot back, "Don't be so silly." She

He kept trying to convince Mrs. Mills his weapon was real.

183

pushed the would-be robber's gun aside. "That's a toy gun. Just go away."

Mom Mills had been in this situation dozens of times before, when her own young ruffians confronted her with broom handles and sticks, demanding that she raise her hands and surrender. "I was in my own little world," she remembers about her bank showdown. "I spoke to the robber as if he were one of my boys."

She was right. The "gunman" was holding two metal pipes taped together to look like a shotgun. He kept trying to convince Mrs. Mills his weapon was real while the teller hit the silent alarm and the police arrived.

He couldn't even convince her that he was "old enough to know better."

DUMB CRIMINAL QUIZ NO. 797

How well do you know our legal system? (The young and the dumb love it.)

In New York City, what percentage of juveniles arrested for misdemeanors never go to court?

A. 37 percent.

B. 91 percent.

C. 8 percent.

D. 76 percent.

The correct answer is B. A whopping 91 percent of those arrested youngsters never see a judge! No wonder they don't take the law seriously.

185

Usin' Your 'Ead

(Australia)

Now we venture to Queensland in the Land Down Under for a comically bizarre tale.

Police officer Colin Walker received a call from dispatch about two suspicious men walking around, looking into parked cars. When he arrived, Officer Walker turned off his lights and parked in an alley between two houses, from where he could clearly see the two men. Something was awry. One man was walking backward, dragging the other toward the passenger side of a running 1958 Oldsmobile. As any moviegoer might be wont to say, *What's wrong with this picture?*

"Police! Don't move!" shouted Walker, his weapon drawn. As the officer approached the suspect, the man on the ground was moaning. He had a very large purple and red knot on the top of his head. Officer Walker

quickly frisked the first man for weapons, then handcuffed him to the passenger-side door handle of the still-running car. Next he attended to the man on the ground who was now sitting up.

"Just take it easy man, an ambulance is on the way," he told him. "What's going on here?"

Seeing the cop and hearing more sirens on the way, the man's nerve broke and he began to babble.

"We were going to rob the owner of this bar, who always carries a lot of cash on him, but I don't have a car so we—"

"Shut up, you idiot!" screamed his partner.

"Go ahead, mate, you were going to rob this bar owner but you needed a car and—"

"And since I don't drive, I told Aldo if he'd drive I'd cut him in for half. Well, he said he'd drive but we'd better steal a car in case someone saw us pullin' off and uhh—"

"Well, what happened to you? Did you two get into a fight or something?" Walker quizzed.

"Oh no, nothin' like that. See, we was walkin' about lookin' for a fast getaway car when we spotted this big ol' V8 Olds. So Aldo popped the hood and hot-wired it. After it started, he was lookin' at the engine with his hands up on the on the hood, sayin', 'Man, they just don't make 'em like that anymore.' Well, I stuck me 'ead

187

in to grab a peek just as he was slammin' it shut. That's the last thing I remember."

Officer Walker shook his head in disbelief. "You blokes might want to consider getting into some other line of work when you get out of jail."

So ends the blunder from Down Under.

Pride Goeth Before the Brain

77

(America)

An officer in Nashville, Tennessee, responded to a burglar alarm at a convenience store. Within moments his K-9 partner had located the perpetrator, but the officer could not figure out how the man got into the store. When he asked, the culprit led him to a small missing windowpane. The officer could not believe the man could get through such a small opening, but brainus minimus insisted that he had. The more the officer protested, the more the crook insisted that he was "that good."

Finally the break-in artist insisted that if the officer didn't believe him, he should take a look at the restaurant three blocks away. "I broke in there earlier tonight . . . through an even smaller windowpane!"

78 The Early Bird Gets Nothing but the Worm

(Canada)

It was a winter holiday, and the whole town of Burnaby was sleeping in, including the shop owners. Even the convenience-store owner was about forty minutes late to open, knowing that no one would be in for another couple of hours.

No sooner had he opened the doors, however, then a young man wearing a ski mask strode in. The owner wasn't alarmed. It was cold outside, and many Canadians are accustomed to donning ski masks, even when they're not committing a crime.

When the man in the mask produced a gun and demanded money, however, the owner finally understood he wasn't looking for the ski lift. The store owner explained that he didn't have much cash on hand because he hadn't had any customers yet. The would-be robber just kept waving the gun around, so the owner gave him the fifty dollars from the change drawer. Then, as the dummy turned to leave, the owner coolly popped him in the head with a baseball bat before calling the police and an ambulance.

"I would've let him go," the owner told police, "but he insisted on robbing me. I don't know why he tried to do it at opening on a holiday. Maybe he never had a job, so he just doesn't know about these things."

The convict would have been wise to hang on to his ski mask so that he could stay warm while chilling out in the cooler.

Safer than Cash

(Democratic Republic of the Congo)

A good job is hard to find in Kenshasa. Millions of people compete for a handful of jobs, so most workers are very conscientious. That was certainly true of a worker named Abdulai. For three years, he had come to work on time and with a smile. Manning a cash register on the deadly night shift, Abdulai had pulled down double- and triple-time wages. He had also received every raise possible for his perfect work record.

One night, however, Abdulai came down with something—chills, fever, weakness. He dragged himself to work anyway, determined not to break his record. Halfway through his shift, however, Abdulai had to call a cousin for help. The kind relative was more than willing to man the register while Abdulai rested in the back room. After his nap, Abdulai felt strong enough to relieve his cousin and finish the shift on his own.

Abdulai felt much better when he reported for work the next evening—until he saw his enraged boss and the two police officers. It seems that someone had pocketed two money orders on Abdulai's shift and used them to pay a traffic fine! Abdulai wasted no time in taking them directly to his cousin, who at that moment was returning from court . . . and was immediately returned there.

The Running of the Fools

(Spain)

Pamplona is famous for its Running of the Bulls, an annual festival in which wild herds of people run through the streets of town chased by charging bulls. Now, thanks to a couple of dumb criminals, Spain adds to that distinguished event "the Running of the Fools."

Enrico Cortez and his brother Miguel were thieves with a plan to rob a merchant who had been collecting money for a sick child. Knowing the store would be closed for the festivities, the Cortezes figured they would break in during the festivities and escape by stepping out into the street and blending in with the milling crowd. What could be easier?

Everything was going exactly as planned. They quickly entered the targeted shop and found the locked metal box containing the cash. Then came the unexpected

"El Toro! El Toro is coming!" came the collective shouts. Too late.

sound of rattling keys at the front door. With no time to think and nowhere to hide, the brothers grabbed the money box and ran. And run they did—out the back door, onto the street, and directly into the path of a crowd of frantically screaming people.

"El Toro! El Toro is coming!" came the collective shouts. Too late. The two wild-eyed brothers were mowed down by running hordes of people. Twenty seconds later, the bruised and confused Miguel watched his big brother Enrico rise unsteadily to his feet, only to be hooked by the seat of his pants on the horns of a very enraged bull. He was tossed about fifteen feet into the air where he spun in awkward gyrations. Gravity pulled him back down headfirst on the unforgiving cobblestone, just in time for the second wave of runners following the bull to trample him again.

After the dust settled, the heartless pair were scraped up and turned over to the police. As for the trampled money box, it had miraculously landed in the doorway of the merchant who had been collecting for the child.

As you can see, the pain in Spain falls mainly on the brain.

Free Mow, No Tow

81

(Australia)

Lyle Hannibal was just a regular bloke who lived in Sydney: He went to work, kept his nose clean, and paid his taxes. Like many Australians, though, Hannibal liked to quench his thirst with a cold brew. This was exactly what Hannibal planned to do on a hot summer Saturday, until his wife informed him that what he *really* needed to do was mow the lawn.

Hannibal rifled back the perfect excuse: "Can't, dearest. The mower's broken."

"Then get it fixed, luv," Martha fired back.

Hannibal awkwardly loaded the mower into the trunk of his car and set off for the shop. He hoped the diagnosis would be serious, involving parts being ordered or perhaps even waiting for a motor transplant. Unfortunately, the mechanic said he could have it running like a top in about two hours. While he waited, Hannibal went to the pub next door to drown his sorrows. Two hours and six beers later, he was headed home with his working mower and a pretty serious beer buzz.

Just a block and a half from his house, Hannibal spotted two police cars with lights on. Two officers were giving a field sobriety test to a motorist. Even in his impaired state, Hannibal realized that this DUI roadblock could become a big problem for him. He would be stopped, and he would fail the test. More importantly, his wife would kill him.

That's when Hannibal had his stroke of genius. He pulled the car over half a block from the roadblock, coolly unloaded his mower, and began mowing a total stranger's front yard.

After about forty-five minutes, the two officers loaded up their gear, took down the roadblock, and headed back to the station just as Hannibal, sweaty and tired, was finishing the front yard. That's when the owner of the house came out to confront Hannibal.

"Now that you're done with the front, you can start on the back." The man then got out his wallet and showed Hannibal his nice police badge. Hannibal had chosen the yard of an off-duty deputy for his hideout.

Plastic Dummy

82

(America)

A Cincinnati woman was waiting in an ATM line when a young man grabbed her purse and ran away. As he ran, however, he dropped a VISA card.

The officer responding to the call thought the card was probably stolen, but he ran a check on it anyway. Lo and behold, VISA said the card had not been reported stolen and supplied a photo from surveillance-cam footage of the last man who had used the card. His appearance matched the description given by the victim perfectly, right down to the clothes he was wearing.

The officer was astonished, but the dumb criminal wasn't. "I was wondering when you'd come for me," he told his arresting officers when they showed up at his door.

83 Married, with Problems

(England)

A string of post office robberies in 1994 and 1995 had British police stymied. A lone gunman would appear in a town's post office, demand and get his cash, then disappear without a trace. Within two years the fleet-footed gunman had made off with more than fifty thousand pounds.

What police didn't know at the time was that the lone gunman was not actually alone. True to the old saying, "Behind every successful man, there's a woman," the robberies were the handiwork of the husband-and-wife team of Bob and Betty Houlihan. Bob did the front-line work—carrying the gun, threatening violence, and carrying the loot to the car. Pedal-to-the-Metal Betty drove the getaway car. Together, they were the most successful crime team in the United Kingdom—until one fateful day in September 1995.

It happened at a small post office on the outskirts of London. As usual, Betty pulled up and parked. Bob jumped out and headed off for another day at the (post) office. He pulled his gun, threatened to shoot everyone, and demanded money. The postal clerk gathered up all the cash and shoved it across the counter. Everything worked like the usual clockwork. Crime was so easy it was almost becoming boring to him.

Then Bob walked out to hop into the car and noticed something different. Betty was not in the car. The engine wasn't running. Looking off to the side, Bob finally saw his wife looking very perturbed.

"Let's go, Betty," Bob snapped.

"Can't, Bob. Sorry." She made no move to leave.

"Let's go, Betty. *Now*!"

"Don't start with me," she said. "I just stepped out to walk Timmy, and I locked the keys in the car." Bob looked down at the couple's Jack Russell terrier. Timmy just barked and wagged his tail. And that's when the police apprehended them. The dog catcher came for Timmy, and Betty and Bobby argued all the way to the jail.

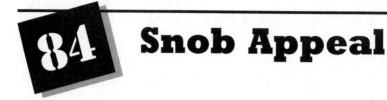

Snob Appeal

(France)

The city of Paris boasts some of the world's finest hotels, catering to such notables as heads of state, oil magnates, and movie stars. Such guests usually expect individualized service, fawning attention, and total luxury. And the guests at these elegant establishments have learned to be patient with millionaire whiners and demanding divas.

Sheik Abdul Lama Ra appeared to be just such a spoiled brat when he first arrived at his Paris hotel. His entourage made a clamorous entrance, with the sheik wailing about lost luggage and demanding that the bellhop fetch a tailor immediately. But he also stuffed twenty francs into the bellhop's hand, an action that immediately disposed the bellhop in his favor.

Over the next few days, the staff realized that there

was something very odd about the sheik. His demands were outrageous—a bowl of yellow M&Ms (just yellow!), a vintage wine flown in from Bordeaux, etc. But his tips were huge, and his open enjoyment of the services rather touching. He lacked the jaded quality the staff had come to expect from typical guests. And typical guests never guzzled their wine and enthused, "Hey, this stuff is great!"

Other evidence gradually began to mount that all was not as it seemed with the sheik. "Without his turban and sunglasses," the valet reported, "he looks like an English house painter." Several employees noticed that the sheik's accent would occasionally slip. And the desk clerk noted a number of phone calls to a working-class neighborhood of Brighton, England.

Then came the day when the seventy-year-old woman from Brighton appeared, asking for the sheik's room.

"Is he expecting you, madam?" the manager asked.

"Well, he would be, wouldn't he? He invited me here himself. I'm his mum."

The manager simply nodded and escorted her upstairs. Sheik Howie's jaw dropped to see his mum with the manager, but that consummate professional only let him squirm for a moment. "If your mother would like to order dinner now, sir," he said, "we could serve you here in your suite."

The staff realized that there was something very odd about the sheik.

Howie swallowed, losing his accent entirely. "That would be lovely."

"Then, if you would be so kind, sir, I need to speak to you downstairs . . ."

Sheik Howie and his mum enjoyed an elegant dinner compliments of the hotel manager. He put his mum on her train back to Brighton, England. Then he surrendered to authorities and began the long process of paying off his hotel bill of seventy-six thousand francs.

85 Party Pooper

(Canada)

Whoever first pointed out that "love hurts" probably spoke from painful romantic experience—but nothing close to that felt by an ardent but especially foolish young criminal in Vancouver.

It began the evening one of the city's nicer restaurants threw its annual Christmas party. The event was closed to the public, but this particular young man managed to make it in uninvited. He was sweet on a young woman who was attending the party and he wanted to see her. It turned out, however, that she did *not* want to see him. An argument ensued between the two, and several guests came to the young woman's defense.

The uninvited guest was politely asked to leave. He responded less politely by throwing a punch, and the "discussion" moved outside into an alley. There the fisticuffs suddenly ceased when the gate-crashing Romeo pulled a .357 Magnum and threatened the whole crowd with it.

You do not argue with a .357 Magnum, especially when it's being held by a very shaky, very upset young man in love, who just got shot down in flames. The crowd slowly backed away without saying a word.

Romeo thought he was in control of the situation now, so he got a little cocky. He began to tell the whole group what he thought of them and of the girl who had just jilted him. After a stream of very unkind remarks, he apparently decided that he had given the crowd a piece of his mind and could put away his "piece." Like a cool Canadian "Dirty Harry," he jammed the huge pistol into the waistband of his pants, and *Kaboom*!"

The emergency surgeons worked hard, but they could not undo all the damage that had been done by Romeo's cool move.

Needless to say, that was the last bullet he would ever get to fire.

Out of the Woods

(America)

One cold winter's night in Ohio, a pair of police officers were called to a gas station robbery in progress. They immediately captured one crook, but another escaped into the snowy woods behind the station. While back-up units were on their way to help with the search, one officer left the scene to transport the prisoner while the other prepared to drive the bad guys' car to the impound lot.

He never made it to the lot. Instead, he walked into the police station fifteen minutes later with the second bad guy in tow.

"I followed you toward the station for a couple of blocks," he explained to his surprised partner. "But then I thought of how cold it is, and I thought maybe this guy was ready to come out of those woods. I drove back to the gas station (in the bad guys' car) and honked the horn. The bad guy ran out of the woods, jumped into the car, and said, 'Where've you been? It's colder'n hell out there!'

"I just said, 'You're under arrest.' "

A Woman and Her Purse

(Australia)

In the parking lot of a large mall just outside Brisbane, a young woman was strolling to her car pushing a shopping cart. Her purse dangled from her shoulder. She didn't hear the car creeping up on her from behind.

Now, it's not unusual for a car to be moving slowly through a parking lot—maybe they were just looking for a space. On the other hand, maybe the car was actually a stolen vehicle with four out-of-control teenagers out on a joyriding crime spree. And maybe those teens had decided to sidle up to the woman as closely as possible so that one of the dudes in the back seat could lean out the window and grab the handle of her purse.

Such was the case. The girl driving the stolen car floored the accelerator and aimed at the lady's back. The boy in the back leaned half out of the window. *Whoosh*!

The car brushed right by the woman's shoulder as a hand deftly lifted the purse. The teens laughed as they sped away, not knowing that this victim was not about to give up her handbag that easily.

The car screeched to a halt to avoid colliding with a car crossing in front of them. That's when the woman caught the boy in the back seat by his long hair. She began to pull him out the window of the car by his hair while he screamed in pain, *"Go, go, get out of here!"* No go. They had hot-wired the ignition of the car to steal it, but now the car had stalled. That's when the three boys jumped ship and ran, with the one still clinging to the woman's purse.

The girl was struggling in the front seat. She had the driver's side door open, but the strap of her own purse had gotten wrapped around the little knob used to adjust the seat, and she was trying to pull it free. But when the victim came around and began pummeling her with her fists, the driver simply abandoned her purse and made a run for it.

Imagine the officer's surprise when he arrived at the scene of the crime and the victim presented him with one recaptured stolen car and a photo ID of one of the culprits.

The moral of the story? Never come between an Australian woman and her purse.

88 Be Careful What You Invent

(England)

George Musgrave was ticketed not long ago by a traffic bobby in London for parking on a yellow line. It was a minor offense and a minor fine, but there was something unusual about the crime.

You see, George Musgrave was responsible for the very existence of the yellow line. In 1947, George had suggested that the Motor Vehicle Department use yellow lines for no-parking zones and the like. It was all part of a road-safety competition.

George's suggestion netted him a three-pound prize.

George's parking ticket cost him a thirty-pound fine.

Adios, Amigos  **89**

(Mexico)

In a small town outside of Mexico City, three would-be bank robbers devised a master plan. One of the men had gathered some information about the inner workings of the bank; he even had a floor plan with an underground map of the area. The plan was to burrow beneath the street, tunnel under the bank, and, with cutting tools, torches, sledge hammers, and picks, break into the bank vault from the tunnel below. It *seemed* like a pretty good plan.

After working several nights, they finally reached the underground flooring of what they believed to be the bank. With victory close at hand, they began drilling, hammering, and cutting with an acetylene torch. Things were going faster than they had hoped and it wasn't long before entry through the floor seemed certain. But there was about to be a problem.

Unbeknownst to our three amigos, their map had been reversed. Either they drew it up backward or they had held it upside down, for just as the torch was cutting through the last of the flooring, they heard sizzling and smelled smoke. The torch had ignited the first of thousands of cases of fireworks stored in a warehouse. The inevitable explosion leveled the building and damaged several others in the area. The bank on the opposite corner suffered only minor damage.

The robbers survived and were captured, tried, and convicted. Maybe they would have been better off with a compass.

The torch had ignited the first of thousands of cases of fireworks stored in a warehouse.

90 A Hansel and (Burp) Gretel Story

(Germany)

The city of Munich loves its beer—and for good reason. Generations of the world's greatest brewmeisters, as well as the world's largest Oktoberfest celebration, call Munich home. With such a frothy history, though, it's no wonder that Munich has its share of alcohol-related crime. Some citizens, in fact, take their beer more seriously than the law—like the three thirsty citizens who thought they could have their beer free and drink it, too.

They broke into the brewery through a wall-mounted vent and headed straight for the large coolers in back, where each man grabbed a couple of cases. Then they all headed for the back door . . . blissfully unaware that they had tripped a silent alarm. An approaching officer shouted for them to halt as they came barreling outside. But they just dashed faster, not noticing that one of the

216

beer cases had split and that cans of beer were spilling out behind them.

Like Hansel and Gretel in the forest, the officer and his back-up then followed a trail of cans down the street and up the steps of a house, where an old lady let them in. A can of beer near the basement door told them where to go next. With guns and flashlights drawn, the officers followed the trail into the dark basement, where they found the three dummkopfs about half a can deep into their drinking binge.

Bottoms up, guys!

91 Pickpocket Panic

(Italy)

Tourists are always warned about the pickpockets in foreign countries. It doesn't matter if you're in Picadilly Circus or on the beach in Pago Pago, the stories of the pickpockets' exploits are by now mythical. In Rome, one such legendary pickpocket domain is the Spanish Steps. The beautiful steps climb upward forever, and in the morning sun or by moonlight, the steps and their surroundings have inspired many poets, film makers, and pickpockets.

It was on just such a day that Mark Burton and his new bride strolled around arm in arm, very much in love. Burton was blissfully suspended in time until the hand brushed his rear. He hoped it was Fran, his bride. When he felt the wallet go, he was hoping it wasn't Fran. They always say the first argument is about money.

218

It wasn't Franny. It was a fourteen-year-old boy who darted up the steps. Burton gave chase. The boy sped up. Burton cranked it up two notches and forced the boy into the corner of a landing, where he tripped him up. The teen gasped for wind as Burton stood over him, pleasantly warmed up and ready for more.

"Wanna race down? Last one to the bottom goes to jail."

Burton grabbed his wallet back and waited for the policeman who shuffled up the steps, huffing and puffing. The teen had picked the wrong guy—Mark Burton is a veteran marathoner.

DUMB CRIMINAL QUIZ NO. 714

How well do you know the dumb criminal mind?

In India, police found a drunk who had climbed over a fence at the zoo to pet a Bengal tiger. Why was he not arrested?

A. He was the zoo's director.

B. He was the chief of police.

C. There wasn't enough of him left to arrest.

D. He used to own the big cat.

Unfortunately, the correct answer is C. As Tarzan says, "It's a jungle out there."

Welcome to the Waltons

92

(America)

It all started when an elderly couple in Billings, Montana, hired two teenage boys for a couple of days of summer yard work. Seven months later, when the two boys were scheming for a way to make some cash, they remembered the couple. An old man and an old woman living alone—an easy mark. Or so they thought.

The two punks parked well away from the house and sneaked up in the dark. They kicked down the kitchen door with little concern about the noise, assuming they could handle the old coots physically, even if they were heard coming.

As they started up the stairs, however, they ran into the old couple's daughter, who had been awakened by the sounds in the kitchen. Her screams woke up her husband, as well as another of the old couple's sons-in-law and his two sons, including weight-lifter Bobby.

That made two grandparents, a daughter, two sons-in-law, and two grandsons—all pitted against a pair of scrawny teenagers. By the time the seven family members were pried off, the punks were bruised, bitten, and scared to death. The police had rescued them from a nice, old-fashioned Thanksgiving at Grandma and Grandpa's.

What a couple of turkeys!

I Scream, You Scream

(United Kingdom [Isle of Man])

Between Wales and Ireland in the Irish Sea lies a tiny island known as the Isle of Man. It has the longest continuous parliamentary form of government in the world. The Isle of Man is also the home of the Manx cat. It is a beautiful little island, with white cliffs rising up out of the green sea, lovely rolling farmland and sand beaches covered in stones worn smooth by the tides.

Every summer the island hosts professional motorcycle racing. Literally, the one road that circles the whole island is the race course. Farmers pile up haybales on hairpin turns to pad the crashes of the cyclists, and thousands of fans invade the island for a week of squealing tires and shrieking engines.

This particular year there was a particular Italian racer entered, whom we'll call Giuseppe. Giuseppe was easily angered and had a reputation on the circuit as a hothead. He had a tendency to push the bike too hard in the corners. So it was no surprise to the other racers when Giuseppe totaled his bike on the first day of time trials.

Giuseppe's greatest nemesis and arch rival on the tour was a German, Klaus. Klaus couldn't help but smile broadly when he saw the "Scratched" on the leader board beside Giuseppe's name. Words were exchanged and, had it not been for their crews, they would have come to blows.

It was also no surprise when Giuseppe blamed Klaus for his crash, claiming his bike had been tampered with. His accusations were groundless and the officials dismissed them immediately, but Giuseppe would have his revenge.

That night Giuseppe partied with the fans who were camping all over the island. At campfire after campfire, Giuseppe drank the wine at each one, playing, in almost operatic style, the fallen hero, the sad clown. He was just drunk enough and mad enough now to do something really stupid.

It was two in the morning when Giuseppe finally stumbled into the alley of garages in the business district of Castletown. Klaus and the German contingent were staying on the next street over, but their bikes were in one of these garages. Giuseppe found the German insignia.

Without hesitation, Giuseppe put his fist through the glass pane of the door and opened the door from the inside. He was still wearing his leather motorcycle gloves so the shards of glass didn't leave a scratch. He fumbled in the dark, groping for a light switch, but found none. Feeling his way forward, he bumped into something about knee high that felt like a tire. He thought it was the front tire of a motorcycle, so he pushed it hard to knock the whole bike over. But when he did, it *kicked* him real hard. Giuseppe went down howling as "the thing" caught him square in the chest. Then the lights came on.

There sat Klaus and three crew members eating ice cream. Knowing Giuseppe, Klaus had a feeling the idiot would try something. They didn't turn Giuseppe in to the officials, even though by the time they got done with him, Giuseppe wished that they had.

Peekaboo, We Saw You!

(Japan)

Unfortunately, it would seem that the dumbest criminals in Japan are Americans. A retired United States Air Force security policeman stationed in Okinawa believes he has evidence to support that claim.

It was Christmas Eve back in 1979, and the security officer on watch was making his rounds around the base. Walking past the base bank, he decided for some reason to take a peek in the window. He cupped his hand against the glass and was shocked to see another face right up against the same window on the inside. Both faces jerked back quickly.

The patrolling officer called for back-up. Within minutes other security officers had secured the bank and the three thieves inside.

It turns out the bank robbers were airmen who had

planned the job for months. They had all applied for and taken leave. They all had their passports, leave papers, and cash and were booked on a Christmas morning flight. They had been mere moments away from escaping with the base payroll—almost a half a million in cash—when one of them happened to look out the window.

"Why did you do it?" the officers had to ask.

The nostalgic thief answered, "I wanted to see the Christmas Eve sky."

We presume he didn't see a tiny sleigh pulled by reindeer and he didn't see the wise men following a star. But he did see his future—in jail.

A L'il Chef Will Do Ya

(England)

There's a restaurant chain in England known as the L'il Chef, identified by signs that display a funny little chef character. He's three-dimensional, made of tin, and stands about four and half feet high. He's perched atop a sign which tops out about thirty feet above the ground on the roof of each restaurant.

L'il Chef is like the English cousin of the American "Big Boy." Like his American cousin, L'il Chef has been the target of many student pranks and much vandalism. Poor L'il Chef has suffered everything from a painted mustache to chef-napping.

One Saturday night a few college students who had downed several pints of ale decided that L'il Chef was probably bored and bloody well tired of seeing the same

L'il Chef was having the time of his life.

sights day-in and day-out. So they liberated him from the rooftop.

They carefully disconnected the bolts holding him to the sign and made off with him. Riding back to school in the vandals' old Triumph convertible, L'il Chef was having the time of his life. He was standing in the back seat of the convertible with the top down and the wind flowing through his painted hair.

The students made it back to their dorm. Their only mistake came the next afternoon when the students decided to take L'il Chef rowing. That's where they met the dean, who was escorting a prestigious alumnus around the campus. His heart sank as the still-hungover students rowed by with L'il Chef on the prow of their boat.

You see, the alumnus watching from the river bank had amassed a fortune as the CEO of L'il Chef restaurants. He actually took it quite well though, since he had almost been expelled when he attended the college for a similar incident. When the big cheese of L'il Chef was a senior, he had helped kidnap and barbecue a rival college's pig mascot.

He saw the chef-napping as an improvement in the ethics of the students. At least the boys hadn't cannibalized L'il Chef.

Stage Fright

(Canada)

A man entered a market in Windsor, Ontario, carrying a bag and a rifle. After demanding that the clerk fill up the bag, he realized that he had not pulled his ski mask down over his face. In his nervousness he pulled the mask down too far and could not locate his eyeholes. Another yank, and it popped off onto the floor. Bending to pick it up, he looked directly at the surveillance camera. Then he had to set his gun down to use both hands on the mask. The guy made a run for it when he finally got the mask on right, but at that point the cops were pulling up. They helped him take the mask off.

97 The Un-Love Bug

(America)

Three dumb criminals were on their way to robbing a bank in Alabama. Spotting a VW bug in the parking lot, they decided to steal it for their getaway car. One of them broke out a window and hot-wired the car while the other two robbed the bank.

The two robbers came out waving guns and bags of money. They jumped into the VW and the driver, who was acquainted with a totally different gear-shift pattern, slammed the bug into reverse and floored it. With the bank employees and, now, the police looking on, the three stooges' car screeched off backward—right under the high bumper of a big truck. Everyone laughed as the stooges frantically shifted gears and burned rubber as their back wheels remained wedged under the truck. They were going nowhere—except straight to prison.

cixelsyD revirD eraweB

(England)

A traffic officer patrolling just outside of Chester spotted a car going well over the posted speed limit. He tailed the car for more than a mile—long enough to clock its exact speed. The driver never slowed down, until the officer pulled him over. Then he seemed genuinely bewildered.

"Didn't you know you were doing fifty-two in a twenty-five speed zone?" the officer asked.

"Oh, no, sir," he answered. "I respectfully disagree. I was doing fifty-two in a fifty-two-mile-per-hour zone."

The officer finally established that this gentleman suffered from dyslexia. He was genuinely reading the speed limit backward and obeying it to the letter. The officer let the driver go with a warning and a bit of advice: When in doubt about the speed limit, always choose the lower number if you have a tendency to reverse the digits!

Dope on a Rope

(Kenya)

Poaching endangered species is a particularly offensive crime. The incredible waste of killing a huge white rhino, then grinding its horn into powder for use as an aphrodisiac, is utterly insane.

Three village men in Kenya had set many traps in the game preserve. Now it was time to check the traps. But two of the poachers got cold feet. The government had recently increased patrols and was dealing severe sentences to poachers.

The third poacher stormed off into the jungle alone, cursing his compatriots. His partners had set most of the traps and they had the map. But on he went.

The poacher was trodding a well-worn path when suddenly he was flying through the air. His gun sailed out of his hands as his ankles were cinched in rope. The

The near-sighted rhino was barreling down on the hanging poacher.

poacher was trapped in one of his partners' traps. Without a knife, he could not loosen the rope that bound him.

That's when he saw the rhino. The near-sighted rhino was barreling down on the hanging poacher, who somehow managed to swing just outside the rhino's path. The rhino did not give up, however: He turned and charged again. This went on for an hour until the rhino finally lost interest and left.

The poacher was hanging, limp on his rope, exhausted. That's when he saw the leopard in the tree above him. The leopard wanted to see more man antics, so he swatted at the rope and then he began to chew on it. The poacher was about fourteen feet off the ground, upside down and trying frantically to distract the leopard.

That's when he saw the giraffe. The giraffe mistook the poacher's hair for leaves and munched right down to the man's scalp.

The next morning, a game warden found the pitiful poacher, bleeding, cut, scratched, and bruised. The animals had passed a lovely evening of "turnabout is fair play." At least they didn't grind up the poacher's nose and sell it to a rhino as an aphrodisiac.

You Want Some Fries with That?

100

(Canada)

Carjacking is a terrifying crime, but it's also an incredibly dumb one. Why risk being dragged, run down, or even shot when you could just as easily hot-wire an unattended vehicle? Almost any crime, in fact, seems smarter than carjacking—except perhaps the taxijacking perpetrated by two guys in Vancouver.

It's one thing to hail a cab when you're in a legitimate hurry to get somewhere; quite another when you can't seem to get to jail quite fast enough.

They began by calling the cab to their house, thus leaving their address on record. Then they pulled a knife on the driver, who was still in radio contact with his dispatcher. They directed him through the drive-through window of a hamburger joint, where they refused to pay.

Then they just rode around aimlessly until the police, alerted by both dispatcher and restaurant manager, were able to rescue the driver and arrest them.

We don't know what their lawyer advised them, but they could have pleaded not guilty of having brains!

Daniel Butler's extensive experience in radio, film, and television currently finds him hosting the popular syndicated television show *America's Dumbest Criminals.* He also helped create the Ernest character brought to life by actor Jim Varney. This is his third book, following the *New York Times* best seller *America's Dumbest Criminals* and its sequel *Wanted! Dumb or Alive.* Butler lives with his wife and two sons near Franklin, Tennessee.

Alan Ray co-authored *America's Dumbest Criminals* and *Wanted! Dumb or Alive.* He is an award-winning pop and country music songwriter whose credits include the theme song for the *America's Dumbest Criminals* television show and singer Rick Trevino's recent Top-10 country music hit "I Only Get This Way with You." He also has written special variety shows for National Public Radio. Ray lives with his wife and daughter near Franklin, Tennessee.